Snow White
REWRITTEN

GRITTY NOT PRETTY

RAE MILLER

Printed in the United States.

ISBN 978-0-578-93848-6 Paperback
ISBN 978-0-578-93850-9 Ebook

Cover and book design by Asya Blue Design
Cover photos by Chris Elam Photography

CONTENTS

With deep gratitude I dedicate this book to ~

The ever-present Universal Source of pure love,
light and healing,

My three incredible daughters,

My amazing son and his equally amazing wife,

My precious granddaughter and grandson,

My dear soul sisters,

My kind, loving partner,

And all my beloved canine BFF's (*woof woof*).

To all of you I owe a debt of gratitude for the love you
have shown me. You have taught me what true
love means. I would not be who or where I am
today without you.

I love you forever.

PART ONE

Those who cannot remember the past
are condemned to repeat it.
—*George Santayana*

Those who fail to learn from history
are condemned to repeat it.
—*William Churchill (paraphrase of Santayana)*

TRAUMA AND SNOW WHITE FANTASY

Glass shattering. Screaming. Blood. A five-year-old girl's inner and outer world changed forever. No undoing what I had seen and what I knew from that moment forward. My older brother Ted, had, in an instant of uncontrolled rage, shoved my older sister Viv through a glass door. She was now on her way to the hospital to receive stitches, and, as a highly sensitive child, I felt all of her pain and terror as if the violence had happened to me. I was speechless. Powerless. Frozen in time.

In this one act, my older brother had created my tectonic shift. My sister was big. I was little. *If he can do that to her when he is angry, what will stop him from doing the same to me? Or worse?*

As male anger dominated my home, survival became my constant goal. Day after day, month after month, year after year, I felt terrified, constantly scanning for danger. I could never let down my guard. I was not big or strong enough to fight, so my instinct manifested in flight or freeze. This physiological process happened, flooding my young body with cortisol and adrenaline in response to stress triggers. Too young to cope with my overwhelming emotions, my psyche involuntarily shifted into dissociation. As a result, I do not remember a narrative of my childhood. I only remember brief snapshots in time.

In her book, *Suffering and the Heart of God*[1], Dr. Diane Langberg explains, "As a result of chronic, interpersonal trauma, the child develops vigilance, constant anticipation of danger, chronic anxiety and terror." She goes on to write that, "Dissociation is a thinking process that is often used for coping with chronic abuse. It is a defense mechanism that allows the child to remove itself from the abuse. The child wants to believe the abuse did not happen, so she looks for ways to keep it secret from herself. When the body is trapped in unbearable circumstances, the mind leaves by way of imaginative and trance-like states."

In other words, as a five-year old girl with limited coping mechanisms, I resorted to dissociation to survive the ongoing dangers and violence in our home. Because as a young child I could not make sense of these events, I also was unable to label and store the memories in a logical way. Langberg explains this by writing, "There are essentially no files in the brain of a child where the whole of their abusive experience can be put or understood. If you cannot escape physically, then one possible coping mechanism is to divide the parts of the experience and store them sepa-

---

[1] Suffering and the Heart of God, 2015

rately in your mind, even to the point of rendering them inaccessible – hence amnesia."
It would take me nearly 50 years to put the pieces back together again. This is my story.

Unknown to me, the beginning of my trauma and subconscious programming began on a summer day in the 1960's when I was born on the edge of powerful Lake Superior. I emerged as the youngest of four children, a 7-pound bundle with an abundance of dark hair. From birth I was marinated in a religious belief system which taught that I must obey God, or I would suffer horrifying eternal consequences. I was taught that I was born a "sinner" and because of that irrefutable fact I deserved to spend eternity in a fiery hell separated from God and love. That ominous sense of danger hung over me like a dark, threatening cloud, waiting for God's wrath to strike me if I made a wrong move.

The continual threat of punishment was a very real and powerful motivator for me, ensuring my obedience. The following are only a few of the Bible verses from the New Testament (New International Version)[2] that vividly impressed upon my young mind what God required of me and the consequences if I did not obey. I will also share how I interpreted those terrifying teachings. I do not wish to argue regarding theology or doctrine. I only wish to commu-

---

[2] New International Version Bible, 1973

nicate the severity of emotional and spiritual abuse that was thrust upon me at a very young age when I had no voice and no choice.

"Children obey your parents in the Lord, for this is right. Honor your father and mother, which is the first commandment with a promise, so that it may go well with you and you may enjoy long life on the earth." Ephesians 6:1-4 (*If I don't obey Mom and Dad, I'll die young.*)

"I do not permit a woman to teach or to have authority over a man; she must be silent." 1Timothy 2:12 *(I have to obey men and be silent.)*

"For all have sinned and fall short of the glory of God." Romans 3:23 (*I was born bad.*)

"Not everyone who says to me, 'Lord, Lord,' will enter the kingdom of heaven, but only the one who does the will of my Father in heaven." Matthew 7:21 *(I'll go to hell if I don't obey God all the time.)*

"He *(God)* will punish those who do not know God and do not obey the gospel of our Lord Jesus. They will be punished with everlasting destruction and shut out from the presence of the Lord." 2 Thessalonians 8:9 *(If I don't obey God, I'll be punished forever in hell.)*

"The Son of Man will send out his angels, and they will weed out of his kingdom everything that causes sin and all who do evil. They will throw them into the blazing furnace, where there will be weeping and gnashing of teeth." Matthew 13:41-42 *(If I sin or do evil, the angels will throw me into a blazing furnace.)*

"Do not be afraid of those who kill the body but cannot

kill the soul. Rather be afraid of the One who can destroy both soul and body in hell." Matthew 10:28 *(I have to fear God because he can kill me and send me to hell).*

"But the cowardly, the unbelieving, the vile, the murderers, the sexually immoral, those who practice magic arts, the idolators and all liars – they will be consigned to the fiery lake of burning sulfur." Revelation 21:8 *(If I do any of those bad things or act like those bad people, I'll be in a fiery lake of burning sulfur).*

"If your hand or your foot causes you to stumble, cut it off and throw it away. It is better for you to enter life maimed or crippled than to have two hands or two feet and be thrown into eternal fire. And if your eye causes you to stumble, gouge it out and throw it away. It is better for you to enter life with one eye than to have two eyes and be thrown into the fire of hell." Matthew 18:8-9 *(If I sin, I'll have to cut off my hand or my foot or pull out my eye, so I won't go to hell).*

As a child, I did not know that there was any other way to live. Obedience held the promise of love and safety – which I desperately wanted – while disobedience promised eternal torment. The fact that Jesus had died to save me from that suffering did little to mitigate my terror of a God who had the power to throw both my body and soul into hell. That spiritual programming locked me in an emotional and mental prison for more than four decades, with internal bars just as powerful as any external ones made of steel, with God as my jailer.

Those beliefs were imposed upon me mainly by my

mom, whom I loved very much. Although I believe Mom's intentions were good, the fact remains that I suffered a great deal of pain as a result of her example and teachings. I now understand that the essence of my childhood belief system was abuse in the name of God. From a very young age I subconsciously developed a distorted image of spirituality and of myself.

My mom and dad were a married couple who lived a simple, middle-income existence. I came along as a surprise pregnancy after my older siblings Vivian (Viv), Ted and Seth. Mom gave birth to four children in less than six years. Her passions were God, Jesus, the Bible, praying, attending church, and being a devout Christian wife and mother, in that order.

During my childhood Mom ensured that my siblings and I attended church at least once a week and often more, with Dad enforcing our attendance. Mom's focus excluded anything that did not align with her version of Biblical truth.

Unlike Mom, Dad was adamantly disinterested in attending church or in anything having to do with God and the Bible. While Mom single mindedly pursued God and all things Biblical, Dad passionately pursued hunting and fishing as his religion of choice. Mom's fervor for God was matched by Dad's zeal for blood sports.

As an extreme animal lover, I was intensely averse to watching animals suffer or die. In fact, my dietary preference would have been to not eat meat at all. Contrary to my feelings of strong aversion, Dad predictably displayed great pleasure when involved in his beloved activities. Dad delighted in regaling anyone who would listen to his sporting tales of adventure.

We lived on the edge of Lake Superior until I was two years old. I have no recollection of those first years, only photos of me as a chubby, brown-eyed little one and Mom's description of me as "sunny-natured" and a "darling, easy baby." When I asked her later in life what we did during those years, she stated matter-of-factly, "We revolved around your Dad."

Our family moved when Dad received a work transfer to Illinois. We lived there while I was between the ages of two and five. I have only a few brief snapshots from those years. The first snapshot appears in my mind like tunnel vision, with my sights set on a furry friend running ahead of me through an open area.

In my peripheral vision I registered Ted and Seth playing with a piece of metal pipe attached to a rope, swinging the pipe rapidly through the air. Being happily distracted with the prospect of catching up with my quarry, I paid no heed to the danger. I failed to notice the whereabouts of the whirling pipe until said flying object connected to the back of my head. The pain of the blow abruptly ended my canine mission, and my memory of that day ends there as well.

In contrast to that painful snapshot in Illinois, my next brief memory evokes feelings of delight and giggling. When I close my eyes, I am easily transported back to those happy moments, playing with a neighbor's large dog, Clancy, who outranked me in both size and weight.

I recall looking up at Clancy standing above me, licking my face as I rested on my back on the ground. Although I was effectively pinned by his exuberance and size, I did not feel afraid. Even at that young age, I intuitively knew I was safe with him. I felt a strong emotional connection with Clancy, as I have always felt with dogs.

At the age of five our family moved once again when Dad received the opportunity to transfer to Montana. He and Mom had both been born and raised in Montana, and they had wanted to return to live near family and friends. Dad also had the higher goal of returning for the purpose of indulging his passions of hunting and fishing.

For the first year we lived in a small rental home in town (where I had witnessed Ted's assault on Viv). When I was six years old, the construction of our family home was finished, and we moved to a much larger, rural home. Our closest neighbor was about a quarter mile away and the main town a few miles distance.

Pine-forested hills rose up behind our house to the south and an open, grassy valley sprawled northward for miles, joining with mountains on the northern horizon. One of the mountains was named "The Sleeping Giant" because the outline of the mountain against the sky resembled the body of a giant while sleeping on his back.

For the first time I had my own small bedroom, a space that quickly became my emotional and physical refuge. With a remnant of bright red carpet and enough space for a twin bed, dresser and desk, my room was situated across the hall from Mom and Dad's bedroom and next to Seth's.

During the years of my childhood, I frequently retreated to that space or to the serenity and beauty of nature. My second story window gave me an expansive view of the Helena valley, and I still find a sense of deep peace as I recall that comforting scene. The predictable life-giving energy of nature served as my best friend, always there for me. Stalwart trees standing strong through storms represented resilience and strength. Snowflakes falling delicately against the pines offered a portrait of transformation as they decorated the landscape with shimmering magic. Bright green grass carpeted the valley floor in the spring presenting the miracle of new life. The rhythms of the sun rising and setting gave me a sense of stability and consistency. Nature was my safe place, my escape, where I could always turn for solace.

By all appearances my childhood was idyllic, but appearances can be painfully deceiving. My first brief snapshot of memory comes from shortly after moving into our new home. I descended the plywood stairs to the living room on the main level. Wearing my robe and slippers, I felt happy, like a favored princess.

Mom had summoned all of us children to the living room for Bible reading time, which was common in those days. Ted was sitting in the living room, reclined in a corner chair, reading a book or magazine. Viv, being the oldest and always the one to take charge of her younger siblings, attempted to ensure Ted's attention.

As Viv wordlessly leaned over to yank said reading material from his hands, Ted erupted with a violent kick to her face via his boot clad foot, knocking off her glasses and of course causing her great pain. My happy world turned upside down in an instant. Like the traumatic event when Ted had pushed her through the glass door, I felt my sister's extreme pain. As I stood in shock, silently witnessing another horrifying explosion of rage, I once again registered the terror of what Ted could do when angry, while also being reminded that no one could protect me. So much for idyllic.

By far the happiest time of my childhood occurred during the cherished moments I spent with our family dogs. As is typical of people with highly sensitive natures, I was instinctively drawn to their pure energy. Even though we spoke no words, our emotional connection was strong.

Dad and Mom adopted a very sweet, black mixed breed named Jinx from the animal shelter for Viv. Jinx possessed the heartwarming talent of "smiling" when she wanted something such as love or a morsel of food. At those moments she would wiggle, wag her tail and lift her upper lip to show her teeth, a memory which still brings me much joy today. Our other dog, Sam, was a special breed of hunting dog called a wirehaired pointing griffon.

Mom did not allow dogs inside the house unless they stayed right by the back door in the "mud room" so I spent time with them in that small space or outside. Our yard was not fenced so Jinx and Sam freely roamed the forested hills around our home, and I loved roaming with them.

One day, a year or so after we moved into our new home, Jinx and Sam wandered off and did not return home.

Several days passed without any sign of them until Jinx reappeared with one hind leg injured by a gun shot. I knelt speechless, as she was lying on the lawn with her bloody hind leg. At the same time, I was in awe of how she had managed to drag herself home while in such pain. Jinx was an amazing dog with a huge heart. Since she was still young and therefore stood a good chance of survival, Dad decided to follow the advice of the local veterinarian and have her wounded leg amputated. I was thrilled with his decision. Dad and I shared a love for dogs, for which I am very grateful.

Eventually, Jinx learned to operate very efficiently with three legs, ultimately outliving all the hunting dogs that would call our family theirs through the years. I remember with admiration how her tail spun around rapidly like a propellor as she ran, providing balance in place of her fourth leg. Unfortunately, Sam never did return home. The local ranchers did not take kindly to dogs roaming on their land and Sam was not as fortunate as Jinx.

A heartwarming, happy memory occurred in our new home around the age of five or six. I loved acting out Snow White's fairy tale. A record player in the living room allowed me to transport myself into a fantasy world through a 33-rpm vinyl recording of the story. I became totally absorbed in Snow White's world where, even though tragedy struck, I could count on a happy ending with my loving prince.

I joyfully danced and twirled to the music, carried away by delight as the narrator described Snow White's magical adventures with the animals of the forest and her kind and loyal friends, the seven dwarfs. The tragic moment unfolded as the wicked queen who, deviously disguised as a benevolent old woman, offered her the poisonous apple. Snow White naïvely believed the queen's façade and eagerly took a bite. As I acted out the moment when Snow White bit into the deadly fruit, I fell dramatically on my pink blanket, which Mom had made for me. I then waited in death-like stillness for the magical kiss from my prince, after which we blissfully rode off together into our happily-ever-after.

Although fifty years have passed since those fantasy days in my living room, I can still feel the intense anticipation as my little Self waited for the prince to free her from her trance and carry her away to a perfect life. I feel so much compassion and sadness for her. Compassion because I know that all she wanted was a happy life where she could feel safe and loved. Sadness because she would stay in her trance for almost 50 more years, waiting for a prince to save her, while all along she had the power to save herself.

THE DEEPENING
OF TRAUMA

In order to understand the full depth of my journey since those fantasy days, I have spent years reflecting on my childhood experience. Although I am truly grateful for the blessings of a home, food, clothing, and for how Mom and Dad worked hard to provide those physical necessities, I felt continually starved for emotional connection. What I did not know about myself then is that I was born a "highly sensitive person."[3] That being the case, I exist in the 10-15% of the population who feels emotions and stimulation more deeply than most people and in order to thrive I need emotional connection like fish need water. While material provisions fulfilled my physical needs, they did nothing to satisfy my deep emotional craving.

Mom was physically present in our home and I loved her very much. I wanted to please her and often helped her by doing chores such as cleaning, ironing, cooking and

---

[3] The Highly Sensitive Person, 1998

washing windows. She told me she loved me, and I do not assume to say that was not true. However, I do not remember feeling an emotional connection with her. In contrast, all I remember is how she turned any conversation into a sermon. Like a preacher in the pulpit, she took control and I silently submitted to her passionate prayers or stern monologues about God and the Bible.

I do not remember conversations with Dad or hearing him say he loved me during my childhood. He was silent most of the time. As was true with Mom, I loved him very much and I do not assume to say he did not love me, yet I did not feel an emotional connection with him. I desperately wanted his love and approval and did everything in my power to earn that coveted prize. As with Mom, I did chores and obediently helped him whenever he asked. I sought to be with him whenever possible, even if that meant witnessing or taking part in the slaughter of creatures.

A snapshot in my mind shows me standing next to Dad in the garage, watching and assisting while he expertly performed the gory tasks of cleaning fish on top of the yellow cabinet, his sharp fillet knife gliding through the meat, adeptly separating the prized flesh from the bones and carcass. At times I sat beside him and plucked feathers from ducks, geese and pheasants, trying hard not to focus on the fact that merely hours before those beautiful creatures had been gliding through the air. Then there were the much larger skinned bodies of deer and elk, hoisted upside down from the rafters of the garage every fall. My intense craving for emotional connection with Dad outweighed my revulsion as I witnessed many of those stomach-turning events.

At an early age I intuitively learned that performing, such as being cheerfully obedient, earning good grades and participating in sports could earn Dad's approval, which felt like emotional connection to me. I did anything I could to please him. I was like a little beggar girl constantly sitting at his feet waiting for crumbs of attention or affection to drop.

As Dad was usually away from home working, hunting or fishing, the crumbs were few and far between. When he was home, he was usually emotionally withdrawn with an unhappy expression on his face. His most frequent expression of anger was silence. In the absence of words, I clearly felt his energy.

The truth is I was afraid of Dad's anger as far back as I can remember. I have a vivid memory of watching him throw one of our hunting dogs down the stairs when she failed to respond as he wanted during a training session. I do not remember anything before or after those terrifying moments. I clearly remember the horror and heartbreak I felt as I watched our beloved dog crashing down the stairs, her beautiful body contorting as she fell, yelping loudly in pain. As was true regarding Ted's volatile anger I thought, *if Dad can do that to an innocent dog that I love when she doesn't obey him, then he can do that to me.* I believed I had to constantly be hypervigilant and obey him, or else.

Dad could go from silence to eruption in a split second when he became really angry. In one such instance, when we were having dinner, Ted said something to anger Dad and in an instant, he bolted out of his chair, grabbed Ted and they engaged in a physical fight next to the table. They were very similar in their emotional behaviors and exhibited the same level of volatility.

Based on my performance, good grades and behavior, I was rarely on the receiving end of Dad's anger. But in spite of all my best efforts, I vividly remember one day I directly felt his angry blast. Being a typical teenage driver, I had turned my head to talk to a friend while approaching a stoplight and accidentally rear ended the car in front of me. The sounds of my friend screaming, and the jarring of crunching metal still reverberate in my mind.

That was my first and only accident and I was absolutely terrified to tell Dad. In fact, that day when I returned home and parked the damaged car in the garage, Mom and I cried together as we contemplated the moment when Dad would return home from work. We both knew what would happen.

The terrifying moment of truth came during dinner that night. All I can remember is the overwhelming sensation of terror as I sat in my usual place at the dining room table with Dad sitting next to me. I stared at my plate, stomach churning, unable to choke down a single bite of food.

Dad noticed my uncharacteristic somber mood. My fear was so powerful that I could not force myself to smile and perform cheerily, even for him. He asked me, "Why are you so quiet tonight?" Time stood still as I stared at my plate of food. Sitting across the table from me, Mom remained silent. I was on the verge of either passing out or throwing up as I forced the confession out of my mouth. *I rear ended another car today.* I braced for impact, certain of an imminent explosion. I was not wrong. In the next moment Dad slammed his fist down on the table next to me and yelled, "Can't this family do anything right?" He then launched out of his chair and stormed out the back door. My last memory is the door slamming as I sat shocked and stunned in his angry wake. I do not remember anything after that moment and to my knowledge we did not speak of the incident again.

Although I always felt afraid of Dad, I felt a bit safer around him when he was in a good mood, such as when I had earned good grades or pleased him through some other form of performance. Other predictable times for better humor occurred when he had been lucky in hunting or fishing.

Following the kill of an elk or deer, the family butchering party brought an air of festivity. After hanging upside down in the garage for a week or two, the beheaded, skinned animal carcass would be ceremoniously carried into the house on a piece of plywood and laid like a sacred sacrifice on the altar of the dining room table. We would all take our places for the butchering party while Dad reveled in his victory on that day like a king returning from a victorious battle.

My assigned role was to help Dad, Ted and Seth carve the raw, wild meat. I detested looking at the bloody carcass, trying to block out the mental images of the once-alive beautiful creature that had freely roamed the forest. I concentrated on blocking that visual out of my mind as I dug my knife deep into the raw flesh. The acrid smell was nauseating and overpowering, yet I performed in hopes of pleasing Dad and avoiding his anger.

Dad smoked cigarettes during the entirety of my childhood. At some point in time, I became aware of the dangers of smoking and registered the shocking realization that cigarettes could kill him. Motivated by my deep love for him, I begged him numerous times to stop.

"Dad, smoking can kill you. I don't want you to die. Please, please stop smoking."

In spite of my desperate pleas and sincere desire for him to live, he did not grant my request or to my knowledge even try. He did whatever he wanted, and I eventually stopped begging.

He smoked in the bathroom while he got ready for work every morning, leaving the bathroom reeking of smoke when I would take my turn getting ready for school. He smoked at the dinner table every night while I sat next to him. He smoked in the car when I rode with him. Aside from the fact that his life was at stake, the smell of the smoke made me nauseated.

In my young mind the only conclusion I could draw from his continual and intentional dismissal of my feelings was simple. *Cigarettes matter more to him than I do. I have no choice but to watch him die.* With each inhalation of smoke, I believed he inched a little closer to death.

During my childhood and adult years, Ted and Seth accused me of being Dad's "pet." I always felt the hatred and disdain connected to their claim. I believe Mom also suspected I had special favor with Dad. At times throughout my childhood, she singled me out and recruited me to invite him to church in the hopes that I would have enough influence to convince him to attend with us. While her continual mission was winning him to Jesus, his answer was typically and unapologetically "No." I felt the pain of his rejection each time. I clearly did not carry that much influence.

In my late teens, I attempted to engage Dad in a conversation about God.

"Dad, why don't you believe in God?"

In response to my heartfelt attempt to connect with him and open up a spiritual tête-à-tête he angrily shut down my attempt.

"I'm not interested in a God who always needs to be worshipped." End of spiritual discussion. I never broached the subject again.

Unlike me, Ted and Seth were in trouble fairly often. Ted was typically the instigator, while Seth, being several years younger, followed his lead. I believe Seth was also terrified of Ted's volatile temper and therefore cooperated. When the two of them were together I never knew what might happen. Not only were they both older they were also much larger.

Ted and Seth consistently teased me in cruel and humiliating ways. From a young age I had an overabundance of thick, dark hair on my legs, so they dubbed me "monkey legs". At random times they would derisively yell, "Monkey legs!", laughing hilariously. For that reason, I was very self-conscious of my legs and wore knee-high socks until my mom finally gave me permission to shave my legs when I was 13.

Ted and Seth also found sport in using firecrackers to blow up some of my favorite possessions. I hated them for destroying my cherished treasures, yet I dared not strike back or tell Mom and Dad for fear of their reprisals.

Their typical facial expressions toward me were dismissal, disdain and displeasure. I was frequently on the receiving end of comments such as "stupid, ugly, shut up, go away." I absorbed their statements as truth about myself and my lack of worth. They did not talk to me or want me near them unless they wanted something from me, such as money or doing their chores for them. At those times, they turned on the charm and lured me into their trap. Time and time again I naively believed that if I chose to cooperate, I would gain the ever-sought-after prize of emotional connection and friendship with them.

In spite of how they treated me, like most younger siblings, I desperately wanted them to like me and to be their friend. Inevitably those moments of "friendship" came with a price. When I was around six or seven years old, Seth asked me if I wanted to play doctor in his room. I was rarely offered the privilege of playing with him alone, so I eagerly agreed.

All I remember is laying naked on my back on Seth's

bed staring at the ceiling with my legs spread while he carefully examined my vagina, poking and prodding with his fingers. Something inside me recoiled under his scrutiny. I focused on the ceiling, trying to block out the physical sensations. Per usual I submitted out of fear and the desire for approval.

Another painful memory occurred with Ted and Seth during a family outing in the mountains. We had gone to the particular location that day so Dad could scope out future hunting grounds for deer and elk. We followed his footsteps through a scenic pasture dotted with gopher mounds and surrounded by an evergreen forest. Ted and Seth had brought their guns specifically with the hope of shooting gophers, which they often did for sport. Actually, they shot at just about anything for sport, which was another reason why I stayed away from them.

That day they encouraged me to shoot a gopher, which I had never done. I had not killed any creature before that day. However, on that day my love of animals was eclipsed by my desperate desire to once again win their approval.

I spotted an unlucky gopher sitting on top of a mound. Having grown up in a family that used guns frequently, I knew how to aim and shoot a gun. With my brothers pressuring me, I pulled the trigger and by a twist of fate, the bullet hit the target. Instead of dying instantly, the wounded gopher rolled down the mound, writhing and shrieking in pain, her furry body covered in blood-soaked dirt. I felt her pain and terror as if they were my own while I stared at her suffering, frozen in time. Ted and Seth laughed hilariously, enjoying every moment of my and the poor animal's agony.

Largely due to the fact that Viv was six years older than me, and she had been promoted a grade in elementary school, we lived in different worlds. I always idolized her. Performance was her strong suit and she shone brightly as a straight A student and member of the choir and dance team. She left home for college when I was 11 and returned home from her elite life once in a while. Upon her return, Ted and Seth fawned over her like royalty, freely offering her respect and affection. I understood how they felt because I felt the same way. I also felt heartbroken because I longed for that kind of emotional connection with Ted and Seth.

Unlike Viv, I fought the constant sense of feeling totally and irreparably awkward. I was always above average height and painfully thin. On top of those two overt realities, growing up in Montana during the 70's and 80's did not offer abundant choices for fashion. I was hard pressed to adorn myself in a way that masked my awkwardness. Aside from very limited shopping opportunities, our family did not have much discretionary income and when said income was stretched across four kids, at times I ended up being clothed in my brothers' hand-me-downs.

I do not fault Mom and Dad, nor do I want to complain. I fully acknowledge that having clothes on my back was a lot more than many other children in the world had at that time. However, my innate desire to look and feel pretty, like some of my friends, overrode everything at that stage of my life. A particularly painful and ever-present fashion detail resulted from the fact that my long legs caused my pants to rest at "flood" level long before capris were in fashion, at least in Montana.

I do remember a few outfits, however, in which I felt quite beautiful. I wore one of those fabulous fashion ensembles in third grade, which would have been in 1973. The extraordinary outfit was comprised of purple stretchy bell bottom pants, a bright orange peasant top, and a wide orange belt. I walked to school feeling like the prettiest girl on the planet. Then there was the sparkly light blue dress I wore in my second *and* third grade school pictures. I deemed that luminous fashion statement worthy of not one but two annual photo sessions.

During my middle school years, the Hash jeans became a craze. If any of you were caught up in that fashion frenzy, you know the urgency of procuring a pair of the genuine article. No imitation knock-off brand would do. During one of my shopping trips with Mom when I was fortunate enough to have my own money to spend, I sought out a pair of the genuine article. Being a size 0 and extra tall, my hopes were dashed when my search amongst the few vendors did not result in my heart's desire. When I was forced to settle for a knock-off brand, my disappointment was severe. The counterfeit gold star on the back pocket shouted "inferior." Alas, I felt that imitation was better than nothing at all and I resigned myself to a role of inferiority. As is often the case with human nature and our instinctive response to deprivation, my painful lack of fashion style during my younger years boomeranged during my teen years when I was old enough to earn a paycheck.

As the age of 13 I began working as a waitress at the local pancake house and subsequently secured other part-time jobs throughout high school, from managing the front counter at a fast-food restaurant to working as a secretarial assistant. From the time I earned my first paycheck, I spent my money on as much "high fashion" as I could afford. Pretty dresses, cute shoes, stylish shirts and pants, dazzling accessories. I yearned to shed my awkwardness and transform myself into a creature of beauty and confidence, someone worthy of love and acceptance.

Along with my continual sense of being a fashion faux pas during my younger years, I constantly lived with the painful awareness of my monkey legs. Much to my continual frustration, Mom held fast to the boundary of making me wait until I was 13 to rid myself of the dark, abundant hair. Then, during my 13th birthday party, Mom handed me a pink box to unwrap. While sitting at the table surrounded by my entire family, I opened the package to discover a pink electric women's razor, like a rite of passage. My stomach fell. *This cannot possibly be happening in front of everyone.*

Oh, the humiliation I felt when I unwrapped the emotionally loaded gift with all eyes on me, like opening a box of maxi pads in front of everyone on the day of my first period, as if puberty were not excruciating enough without the spotlight. Ted and Seth gave each other a knowing look, laughing and delighting in every moment of my humiliation.

Being very thin I was a late bloomer. I was still flat as a pancake when other girls in 7th and 8th grade were proudly beginning to display womanly features. To help myself fit in and not attract teasing, I strategically stuffed some Kleenex into my training bra so I could at least *appear* to be maturing like the "cute" girls my age. Tragically, my strategy backfired.

A group of boys approached me outside after school one day. They gathered around me and began groping me, grabbing at my breasts and vagina. One of them managed to reach under my shirt and bra. His eyes grew big as he pulled out a handful of Kleenex, waving it high in the air for all to see. I felt like I had been kicked in the stomach. All the boys roared with laughter and the news spread around the school like wildfire. I never used a bust enhancer again.

By ninth grade, I hit my full height of 5'10". I towered above all the cute girls and most of the boys. Awkward with a capital AWKWARD. At one point my desperation hit an all-time high when I indulged in a home-style perm, courtesy of Mom who knew her way around an Ogilvie home perm. My goal was to transform my boring, lifeless hair into luscious and luxurious curls. Alas, my hopes were dashed when I gazed in horror at the tight, frizzy ringlets. When I finally had to make a public appearance in the dining room sporting my new hairdo, I felt the familiar stab of humiliation. Ted and Seth laughed hysterically and called me poodle.

In spite of my awkward, gangly self, I had a few admirers during my younger years. My true love appeared on the scene in third grade. When Jimmy entered my world, I became aglow with anticipation every day. We were in Mrs. Carpenter's class together, a very kind and grandmotherly woman. He was the fastest boy in third grade, and with my long legs I was his female counterpart. Match made in heaven. Although I was taller than him, that fact did not dampen our attraction.

I do not remember ever talking to him or even hanging out together. Our romantic communication happened mainly through competition in playground games. Sometimes he won. Sometimes I won. Whether we were playing kickball, softball, basketball, or just racing around the playground, our furtive glances communicated volumes. The chemistry was electric.

One day in class I got up the nerve to make a move in order to ascertain Jimmy's true feelings. Those were the good old days of declaring love through a handwritten note, delivered in person. Straightforward and with no room for confusion, my note declared, "I love you. Do you love me?" with two crystal clear choices indicated by a box he could check. YES or NO.

I carefully executed my drop-off maneuver. Despite my extreme nervousness, I nonchalantly walked past Jimmy's desk on my way to the pencil sharpener and stealthily dropped the note on his desk, attracting no one's attention but his. My heart was pounding out of my chest. I have no idea how much time elapsed before he executed the return of my note with matched stealth. All I remember is the note appearing on my desk, as if sent from heaven above.

Unfolding the note, I breathlessly awaited the impending verdict of a love-filled of loveless future. My heart leapt into my throat as I stared in awe at Jimmy's choice. The heavens parted and blessings of pure love showered down on me. There was an unmistakable X in the YES box. Relief and ecstasy flooded my soul. To my knowledge that is the first time I had experienced a male proclaiming love for me.

As I glanced furtively at Jimmy sitting across the room at his desk, the twinkle in his blue eyes and his happy grin told me he was filled with equal delight. Oh, the magic of our emotional connection and the consistent happiness I felt from third through sixth grade with him by my side.

While I was not at school with Jimmy, my canine best friends were my most consistent source of happiness. However, my happiness ebbed and flowed as I periodically lost my fur-friends. Along with Sam, I grieved the loss of four more canine friends during my childhood. Beau, the hunting dog that replaced Sam, wandered off when he was a few years old and like Sam, did not return home. The next hunting dog, also named Beau, died as a puppy when Mom backed the car out of the garage one day and hit him. Our next hunting dog, Cody, was killed by a motorcycle about five years later when she wandered across the nearest highway. Jinx was the only dog left by the time I had reached my late high school years. She died at the age of 11 while chasing the garbage truck. She slipped on the icy road and fell under the wheels. I grieved each loss deeply.

Although my life was characterized by instability in

terms of my canine friends, another part of my life was characterized by extreme stability. Church attendance could be counted on throughout my entire childhood, come rain, snow, sleet or shine. I responded to Pastor Billy's "altar call" at the age of six, which was offered for anyone who had not "invited Jesus into their heart." On that particular Sunday, Pastor Billy did his job well. The prospect of an eternity in hell separated from God's love prompted me out of my pew. I felt terrified as I walked the gauntlet, with everyone's eyes on me and knelt at the altar. I certainly did not want to spend eternity in a lake of fire, and at the same time I wanted "Him" to love me, which was enough to push me past the extreme discomfort of such a public display. After all, I was used to performing for love and approval. I knew no other way.

I entered puberty subconsciously programmed to submit (to God and angry men) out of fear of punishment, while at the same time performing out of a craving for safety and love. I had no model for what a healthy, loving relationship looked or felt like, nor did I understand what love meant. Little did I know that fatal combination made me easy prey, like a lamb to the slaughter.

THE FOG DESCENDS

I graduated from elementary school after sixth grade and entered middle school when I was 12 years old. The adjustment was a bit rough. As is true for most kids, the transition from a smaller, familiar zone where I had known most of the students and teachers was disorienting and scary. However, I soon had my feet under me and proceeded to do what I had always done – perform. As long as I earned good grades, participated in sports, and stayed out of trouble, I could stay safe and even earn occasional praise from my parents.

I made a number of new friends and slowly drifted away from my grade school friends and Jimmy. Middle school was a totally different world than the one we had lived in when we expressed our true love through competition in playground games. There were a lot more boys to flirt with now, and no recess. I never did replace that pure and innocent feeling I had with Jimmy. I wish I could rewind to those days, before the fog descended. Although

I felt consistent fear, sadness and isolation in my home, after the dark fog descended, I would live in a different reality altogether. The dark fog rolled in one day when I was visiting my friend Brenda. How could I have known that I had innocently entered the lion's den? Brenda had a teen brother named Scott who accurately fit that description. He was a popular high school guy, and he was old enough for us to consider him a hero.

I was lying on Brenda's bed when Scott came into the room. Before I knew what was happening, he began kissing me and the sharp metal of his braces cut into my lips. His tongue rolled around inside my mouth. He slid his hand up my shirt and under my bra. At 12 years old I was very naïve, tender and fragile. I had absolutely no idea what was going on. As a sheltered church girl, I knew nothing about sex. All I knew was to not cause trouble, be submissive and not do anything to make a male angry. So, I laid there completely still and did not resist. He slid his hand down my pants, repetitively shoving his fingers in and out of my vagina. I winced in pain. *Submit and stay safe.* I froze. I have no idea how long Scott persisted with his sexual assault. All I know is that during that time my entire inner world shifted, and the dark fog descended. I went from being an innocent girl at a friend's house to feeling violated at a soul level, suspended in time.

Looking back, I know from the moment Scott violated me I began living a "split" life. Unbeknownst to me, one part of me stayed frozen in time, trapped inside by a thick fog, terrified and speechless. The other part of me remained in the light of day, smiling and performing as always. My subconscious mechanism of dissociation once again protected me from a reality for which I had no understanding or coping skills. During eighth grade I had another sexual encounter with a boy my age. We were at a boy/girl party in the basement of a friend's house. At some point, everyone began "pairing" off to make out with someone of the opposite gender. Some of the boys and girls were already officially a couple, which left those of us singles in the awkward position of either conforming or being an outcast. Like most kids, my goal in middle school was to not be an outcast, so I paired off with a boy named Joe who I barely knew. I only remember lying on the floor, squished up against him in a narrow space between the wall and a bed. I submitted to similar treatment as I had experienced with Scott, only not as aggressive. Once again, my instinct told me to freeze and stay safe.

Then, in the summer of 1979, just before my freshman year in high school, I discovered an effective way to distance myself from painful emotions. During summer vacations I typically visited my older female cousin, Lisa, whom I idolized. One particular summer Lisa had a new boyfriend who was in his early 20's and he had a friend who was a senior in high school. My cousin arranged a double date with the friend, Dillon. He was cute, taller than I was and had a charming smile.

I felt nervous and at the same time very cool being

included in their mature social scene, especially drinking beer for the first time in the back seat of the car with Dillon. A few sips in, everything changed. I no longer felt anxious, insecure and awkward. Suddenly I felt really happy. Light as air as I laughed the night away. That evening ended with a replay of my experience with Scott and Joe, the only difference being the alcohol anesthetized my emotions, and I did not feel the same levels of fear or discomfort. Blessed relief.

I entered my freshman year feeling less awkward based on the fact that I was quasi-dating a senior in high school who seemed to like me. The fact that he was from another town added a special air of romantic mystery.

With a growing sense of confidence, I tried out for cheerleading and felt elation when I was selected as one of the five lucky members of the squad. Soon after, a boy named Brad moved from Texas to Montana, and he quickly joined the football team. He was cute and all the other girls in the school liked him.

I felt flattered when Brad singled me out and asked me for a date several weeks later. He picked me up in his cool blue truck and gave me a goodnight kiss in my driveway when he took me home. I was walking on air after that night. Before long we were officially "boyfriend and girlfriend" and as with Jimmy, I basked in the delicious sensation of our emotional connection. My life felt perfect, at least when I was outside of my home.

Soon after we started dating, Brad began saying and doing things that were overtly sexual. One day I performed in front of a school assembly in my short cheerleader skirt. Afterward he smirked and told me, "Whenever your skirt goes up, I can see your 'bush,'" meaning my pubic hair. After that day, whenever he watched me in my cheerleader outfit, he looked at me with the same smirk, stared straight at my vagina and stuck out his tongue, moving it up and down. Although his comments and actions made me uncomfortable, I pushed my discomfort away.

Brad frequently and aggressively pushed for anything sexual, groping my vagina or breasts, whether we were in the school hallway or in private. As I had done with Scott and Dillon, I froze and submitted. I desperately wanted an emotional connection with Brad, so I submitted to everything short of "fornication".

One night when we were making out in his truck, he increased his emotional leverage while pushing for more.

"I love you," he whispered in the heat of the moment.

I had never heard a male say those words to me out loud and my heart leapt into my throat. Brad was offering me what I had craved for so long.

"I love you, too," I whispered.

He quickly capitalized on my earnest profession. "If you love me, you'll have sex with me."

In that moment I felt the extreme internal tug-of-war of choosing between pleasing Brad and obeying God. I knew if I did not give Brad what he wanted I would risk losing his love. On the other hand, if I chose Brad, I would risk God's punishment. In spite of the inherent risk, I chose to obey God simply for the reason that he had the power to send me to hell. Brad did not break up with me, although he eventually found another way to get what he wanted. Not long after sophomore year began, Brad had sex with another girl. I heard of his infidelity through the social grapevine and crushed by his betrayal, ended our relationship immediately. The sensations of shock and pain overwhelmed me as I stood in the hallway listening to a friend telling me that the guy I loved (and who said he loved me) had hooked up with someone else. He had managed to get what I was not willing to give him.

Eventually my heartbreak diminished when later in my sophomore year a popular senior named Allen singled me out. Allen and his friends drank a lot, and I often drank with them. At first Allen was less aggressive than Brad. That changed the night we went to prom together.

We had stayed up most of the night and ended up at a friend's house in the early morning hours. As we watched the sun come up, the effects of the alcohol had waned. Allen tried to convince me that the reason he wanted to have sex with me was because he loved me. As with Brad, my inner battle raged. In spite of Allen's pressure, I once again held my ground and chose to obey God.

At the end of my sophomore year, Allen graduated from high school and we went our separate ways. I entered my junior year with the decision to bypass cheerleading and tried out for basketball instead. I was disillusioned with all the drama involved with being a cheerleader and wanted to try a different angle on performance. Dad loved sports and was pleased with my choice to participate in basketball, which of course felt great to me.

Brad and I got back together during my junior year. He said he still loved me, and being desperate for emotional connection, I believed him. At some point during that year, I went out with him and had too much drink. He drove to a remote mountain road where I had little awareness of what was happening. Some would say we had sex in his car. I say *he* had sex. I was mostly unconscious. I now understand that the reality of my experience that night was rape. In her book *Suffering and the Heart of God,* Dr. Langberg states, "In contemporary legal usage, rape is defined as nonconsensual penetration obtained my physical force, the threat of bodily harm, or at a time when the victim is incapable of giving consent due to mental illness, mental retardation, or intoxication."[4] I certainly fit in the last category.

The next day I woke up with a severe hangover, along with the sickening realization that I was no longer a virgin. I had a vague recollection of lying on the front bench seat of Brad's car with him on top of me, my head hanging upside down out the driver's open door, looking up at the night sky. As I absorbed the truth of what had happened, more of me retreated into the thick dark fog, and I began living more of a split life. I did not speak a word of my trauma to anyone, not even to my friends.

Not knowing anything about sex or relationships for that matter, I continued cooperating with Brad for several reasons. As with Dad and Ted, I was afraid of him. Like Ted

---

[4] Suffering and the Heart of God, 2015

and Dad, Brad frequently displayed anger and emotional volatility, and at times, violence. Several times I watched as he fought with other guys, mercilessly pummeling his opponents. Those times gave me clear information as to what he was capable of when angry, and I registered that fact as I had with Ted and Dad. In fact, he was an emotional replica of them. Also, if I did not cooperate with his demands, he withdrew emotional connection and punished me with angry silence, which felt just as painful as any physical punishment

One night during junior year I went to a school prom with a guy friend because Brad refused to take me. When my friend and I were dancing in the school gym, someone told us that Brad was waiting outside in the parking lot, waiting to beat up my friend when we left. Knowing the seriousness of the threat, we exited through a back door. Thankfully Brad's threat never translated into action.

When Brad was with his group of friends, he would often join them in verbal cruelty. They yelled names at me such as "beak" because of my large nose and "stork" because I was tall and thin. Sadly, their treatment felt normal. I had endured the same kind of treatment with Ted and Seth my whole life.

Around that time, Mom began insisting I wear something other than a t-shirt and underwear in the house when the males were around. The sexual energy in my home became more evident one day when Ted, along with a male cousin, suggested that Lisa and I play spin the bottle with them – strip style. They even offered her a pack of cigarettes as incentive. Even though I felt uncomfortable, I once again went along, wanting to win approval.

Lisa had large breasts, and as we sat in a circle in the forest behind our home, the bottle kept pointing her way. Soon she was sitting next to me with her ample breasts exposed, much to the boy's delight. Not long after, I discovered Ted's stash of pornographic magazines, a finding that shocked my young eyes and left me feeling sad for the women on the pages. I felt even more hypervigilant around Ted after that discovery.

During my last two years of high school, I hung out and partied with my best friend and soul sister, Ella. We had a deep emotional connection from the time we met, which still holds true to this day. Although we rarely talked about the deep pain and struggles in our lives, we understood each other. To cope with our emotional pain, we self-medicated and laughed a lot. She had a sweet basset hound named Muffin, which increased my delight whenever I spent time at Ella's house.

During summer between my junior and senior year, I performed as the maid of honor in Viv's wedding. The night before the wedding I curled into a sleeping bag in Viv's guest room and cried by myself. I thought I was pregnant. The only person I had told was Brad.

While struggling with my emotional dilemma and feeling of isolation, I pondered the reality of how my perfect Christian sister would be marrying the perfect Christian man the next day, while I, on the flipside might be pregnant out of wedlock. Per usual, I performed with a smile on my face throughout the entire wedding weekend and no one was wiser to my emotional crisis. Ultimately my pregnancy scare passed, and I was flooded with overwhelming relief.

My relationship with Brad was a bit rocky after that. He pressured me to take birth control pills. Although I had already crossed the forbidden fornication line, I somehow reasoned that I would add insult to injury by using birth control. I know my logic was confused and yet I felt God definitely would not approve of birth control on top of fornication. Eventually Brad threatened to end our relationship if I did not get the pills. At 16 years old I went to Planned Parenthood by myself and obtained a prescription.

My inner battle grew fiercer and ultimately my religious programming got the upper hand. I could not follow through with taking the pills. I remember having an emotionally charged phone conversation with Brad about God and the Bible.

"I'm not going to take the pills," I proclaimed with conviction.

"Why not?"

"God doesn't want me to. The Bible says so."

"The Bible was written by a bunch of people thousands of years ago. That has nothing to do with us."

"I don't agree," I stated defiantly. "Every word in the Bible is inspired by God."

Our conversation ended in a stalemate and I continued on in my emotional tug-of-war.

I do not remember how I got through my senior year. I

drank a lot and continued having sex with Brad. Whenever I went to church, I slumped in the back pew. God could not possibly love me now. I was a fornicator. I was going to hell for sure.

Dad and Mom did not ask me any questions about my personal life or my relationship with Brad. As long as I continued to perform by staying out of trouble and earning good grades, I did not attract their attention. However, there was a specific incident when I had to involve Mom and she became suspicious.

One day after showering, I noticed some odd little bumps in my pubic hairs. I removed one of them and held it in my hand. Upon examination, I was shocked to see that the dark speck resembled a tiny bug, moving legs and all. I had no idea what the creepy crawly could be, so I showed Mom. She promptly put the specimen in a jar and took me to the doctor. When he informed Mom that I had "crabs," or pubic lice, I had no clue as to what he meant.

Only after he explained how they were transmitted did I connect the dots and understand the doctor's grim prognosis. I had contracted the crabs from Brad. Thankfully, my condition was treatable, and the doctor also told Mom that sometimes crabs can be transferred through bedding or shared articles of clothing. I capitalized on that information and made up a story about a sleepover at a friend's house and the fact that I had borrowed her clothing. There was no further conversation or direct inquiries about the matter after that day.

Several times during those years Mom furtively left

small notes with Bible verses on my dresser, specifically addressing sexual sin and the consequences thereof. Although she clearly suspected sinful behavior, she never addressed the subject directly. Even when she inadvertently discovered a pregnancy test kit in the back of my car, I created the backstory that one of my friends had discarded the incriminating evidence.

During the three years that I dated Brad, he only visited our home once and even then, Mom and Dad did not engage him in conversation. Brad and I sat on the living room couch sipping sodas while Dad focused on the TV and Mom kept herself busy elsewhere. Prior to Brad's arrival she had instructed me that we were to stay in the living room. Brad did not like her mandate because we could not be alone, allowing him to do what he wanted. He never came to my house again.

During senior year, I often conceded to Brad's pressure to do his homework for him so he could graduate. He smoked marijuana frequently and unlike me, did not care about performing to get good grades. As was true of Ted and Seth, he knew how to turn on the charm when he wanted something, and I once again fell for the reward of emotional connection.

After high school graduation I worked as a bank teller during the summers in between my years of college and lived with Mom and Dad. Brad moved back to Texas for work, and I foolishly agreed to stay in a long-distance relationship with him. At that point I still did not want to risk his anger or lose his love. I clearly remember the night before he left, he picked me up in his car and drove to an isolated rural location near a small lake about ten minutes from my house.

He instructed me to take off my clothes and sit on top of him in the driver's seat with my back facing the steering wheel. He pulled down his pants and we had sex in that position. When he felt satisfied, he drove me home. The whole "date" took about a half an hour. No conversation, no dinner, no spending time together other than him achieving his goal. That was the extent of his goodbye.

Later Mom reflected on how she had felt grateful that Brad brought me home as quickly as he did. She said she had prayed he would do so. Little did she know what had occurred in the short time we had been together and why he had returned me so quickly. I protected her from the truth that I knew would grieve her.

In September of 1983 I went to college at the University of Montana. The location, surrounded by hills and mountains with lots of trees, was beautiful. My grandparents had given my parents the lump sum of $5,000 when I was born to hold in trust for my college expenses, for which I am grateful. By the time I reached college age, the money had appreciated to an amount that covered about three quarters of the cost. The rest of the money I earned through working full time in the summer and part time during the school year.

Brad continued living and working in Texas, and I reveled in my independence, frequently running and hiking in the beautiful mountains surrounding campus. I still partied on the weekends with friends, occasionally kissing a few guys when I was drunk, but not engaging in more except one occasion when I was very drunk and succumbed to a one-night stand.

I had infrequent contact with Brad for seven months. In the beginning of our separation, I wrote him letters once a week. He did not once write to me. His sole form of communication with me consisted of phone calls late at night when he was drunk. During those conversations he mostly talked about how much he missed having sex with me. Over the months of our separation the truth slowly dawned. Brad did not love me. By the time December rolled around I knew I did not want to be in a relationship with him.

During Christmas break, I saw Brad for the first time since he had left for Texas. He returned to Montana with the expectation of picking up our relationship right where we had left off. My stomach churned as I worked up the courage to tell him that I wanted to end our relationship.

We sat in the front seat of his car in my driveway as I told him how I felt. I braced for what I knew would happen, and as expected, I felt the brunt of his anger. He told me through angry tears that he hoped someone would hurt me as badly as I had hurt him. At that moment I was able to maintain my clarity and I did not submit to his emotional punishment. Our seven-month separation during which I had not had sex with him had given me enough strength to follow through in the face of his anger.

I returned to college and in February, turned over a

new (or actually old) leaf after a visit from two women who were part of a Christian organization on campus. They knocked on my dorm room door and told me they were doing a random survey regarding students' spiritual beliefs on campus. They inquired if they could discuss the survey with me. They were friendly and seemed harmless enough, so I invited them into my room. They asked me specific questions about the Christian faith, aimed at ascertaining my knowledge of the Bible.

Due to the fact that I had been a regular church attendee throughout childhood, and I had listened to hundreds if not thousands of sermons, I knew all the "right" answers.

After they finished their survey, they asked eagerly, "So you're a Christian?"

I smiled and nodded. "Yes."

They clearly had not guessed that I partied every weekend and had not attended church during the five months since I had arrived at college.

After they left, I pondered their line of questioning and my current heathen lifestyle. All my childhood programming flooded back along with a healthy dose of terror. At that point, based on the resurfacing of religious rules and my associated emotions, I returned to my childhood pattern of attending church. If I claimed to be a Christian, I figured I had better clean up my act and behave like one. My grades had dropped during fall quarter and I refocused my attention on academics as well.

As the months went by, I stayed away from drinking

and guys. My grades improved and I felt happier and lighter. I had no interest in dating and thoroughly enjoyed not being controlled by a guy. My sophomore year in college provided emotional stability, and I delighted in my freedom. I read my Bible and prayed every day. I attended church and Bible study every week.

I felt more freedom and happiness during the next few years in college than I had during my entire life. I was not subjected to angry men and no one was pressuring me for sex. On the outside I appeared to be a smiling, confident, successful college woman. What I did not know was that on the inside existed many frozen Selves, hiding in the dark fog, still terrified and silenced. I had no awareness of the layers of trauma buried within me, creating a split Self.

THE TRANCE TAKES OVER

When Mom and Viv learned that the prodigal had returned to church, they were elated. Now that I was living an upstanding Christian life, Viv began pursuing more contact with me. I soon learned that she had a good friend named Tiffany in her church in Oregon who came from a very reputable Christian family. During the winter of my sophomore year, Viv informed me that Tiffany just so happened to have an eligible Christian brother.

Viv began strategizing as to how she could match her little sister with the eligible bachelor. Her attempt to arrange a meeting for us to go skiing together during the winter of 1985 at a resort near my college town produced no results. To my relief, I did not hear any more about said bachelor for a few months and I hoped Viv's matchmaking scheme was a thing of the past.

Communication with Viv increased toward the end of my sophomore year when I decided to participate in an exchange program during my junior year. I had learned that I could attend any out-of-state college that participated in the exchange program while only paying in-state-tuition. The idea of seeing a new place and living in a different state sounded fun. I shared my idea with Viv who encouraged me to attend a university near her in Oregon. Falling right back into the role of submissive little sister, I went along, hoping that doing so would result in the close relationship with Viv that I had always craved.

Meanwhile, unbeknownst to me, Viv and Tiffany continued to encourage Tiffany's eligible Christian brother to contact me in spite of the fact that I had communicated to Viv that I was not interested in dating. In early June of 1985, at the beginning of my summer break and before my junior year, I had returned to live with Mom and Dad and work at the bank where I had worked during previous summers. One day I received a phone call out of the blue. When I answered, the man on the other end said his name was Edward and that his sister, Tiffany, and my sister were friends.

He informed me that he would be passing through my area in a few weeks and would like to stop by to pay me a visit. Although I was not interested in dating, I agreed to see him. Looking back, I know my decision was completely based on fear and pleasing Viv. If I did not go along with Viv's plan, she might be displeased, and I might lose our emotional connection. Instead of standing up for myself and honoring my feelings, I acquiesced to pleasing Viv.

Viv and I had grown closer as I planned for my year in Oregon, which was something new for me. Although I had always idolized her, I had never felt close to her until then. I did not want to lose that sought after prize. I also viewed her as a Christian role model and mentor, and felt I needed to follow her guidance rather than listening to my own feelings.

True to his word, Edward showed up on the doorstep of Mom and Dad's house in late June, several weeks after our phone call. Being 25, he was five years older than me, nice looking, well-groomed and polite. He was also very nervous, which I chalked up to first date jitters. We did some sight-seeing around town during the day and finished up with dinner at a Chinese restaurant. Our conversation mostly involved talking about our shared faith and topics pertaining to the Bible.

Overall, the day was pleasant enough and at the end we said a polite goodbye and he went on his way. Over the weeks that followed, Viv continued to encourage me in Edward's direction. I wrote him a thank you note for his visit and dinner, and he replied with a similarly proper note.

As I planned for my journey to college in Oregon for my junior year, Dad agreed to transport me and my belongings in his truck. By then he was retired and as had been true my entire life, he capitalized on the opportunity to schedule a fishing trip. After leaving me at the college campus, he continued on to a fishing expedition with a friend at the Oregon coast.

Our travel route to Oregon took us near where Edward

and his parents lived, and we planned to overnight at the midway point of our trip which happened to be in their area. Based on Viv's encouragement, I wrote to Edward to let him know I would be passing through if he wanted to get together during the evening while I was there. I received a return letter in the affirmative. Although Viv clearly wanted more to develop between Edward and me, I still had no desire for anything more than friendship.

When Dad and I arrived at our hotel, I telephoned Edward who then picked me up and drove us to dinner at a restaurant located in a beautiful high-rise hotel poised on the edge of a stunning lake. Having grown up in Montana and having had few meals in nice restaurants, I was in awe. Edward was the perfect gentleman, and once again we mostly talked about subjects related to the Bible.

The overall effect of that evening simulated the allure of the Siren song in Homer's *Odyssey*,[5] when the half-bird, half-woman creatures lured sailors to their destruction by the sweetness of their song. In *Odyssey*, the hero Odysseus, advised by the sorceress Circe, successfully escapes the siren's enchanting song by stopping the ears of his ship's crew with wax and commanding his crew to tie him to the mast of his ship so that he would not be able to steer his ship off course to destruction.

If Odysseus had not been strapped to the mast, he and his crew would have been lured to their death. Unlike Odysseus, I had not been warned of the potential dangers nor had I any defense against the overwhelming lure. Ul-

---

[5] Homer's Odyssey, 675 B.C.

timately, the siren song would only grow louder and more mesmerizing, overpowering any awareness of the serious risks that lay ahead.

After the enjoyable evening with Edward, I continued on my journey with Dad. He helped me carry my few belongings to my dorm room, and then he drove off, leaving me with a mixture of fear and excitement. I knew no one at my new college yet I was determined to make the most of my adventure. I settled into my small dormitory and became acquainted with my new roommate and the campus. Twice a month I visited Viv and her husband, Don, where I soaked up the feeling of emotional connection with family members that I had not felt before.

While visiting Viv and Don, I attended church with them and when I stayed at school, I attended church in my college town. Several guys asked me for dates during that school year and although I agreed to spend time with them as friends, I did not want to be involved in any romantic relationships. Edward and I exchanged letters every month with neither of us hinting at anything beyond friendship. I pursued my academics seriously, earned good grades and sought to live a life of obedience to God.

Christmas break rolled around during my junior year. Viv, Don and I planned a road trip to Montana to be with Mom and Dad. Once again, the travel route would take us through the area where Edward lived. Viv encouraged me to write to let him know we would be passing through their area, and he wrote back, inviting us to his parents' home for a visit.

By then I had heard about his parents, Mac and Marion. They had a stellar reputation as exemplary, benevolent Christians. Mac owned a commercial real estate company and Edward was his right-hand man. He lived near his parents, and although he did not have room in his small home for us to stay with him, he arranged for us to overnight at their larger home.

We arrived one snowy December evening and drove down the long driveway through their forested property. As we slowly drove around a gentle bend, their home appeared in sight. The image was like something out of a fairy tale. A large, Swiss-style chalet outlined in colorful Christmas lights appeared, ensconced in a flocked evergreen forest. Fresh snow draped the magical home and landscape in a white, ethereal glow. Purely breathtaking. The mesmerizing siren song grew louder. Coming from a minimalist dormitory room and a no-frills, middle class home, I had never encountered anything that remotely resembled this dazzling scene.

As if the spell cast by the magical chalet was not mesmerizing enough, the reception we received from Mac and Marion increased the volume of the siren song. They literally greeted us with the sound of a "siren" they had hardwired near their front door which mainly served the purpose of an alarm system. The siren also served the double purpose of welcoming guests. Looking back, I cannot help but feel the irony of the siren as striking. They also met us with shouts of jubilant greetings and hearty hugs. I had never felt such an enthusiastic, loving welcome in all my days. My emotional Self swooned with delight. As they ushered us into their exquisite chalet, the grandeur and splendor of their home was mind boggling.

Everything was dazzling, from the magnificently decorated 16-foot Christmas tree to the shining grand piano to the soaring high ceilings embellished with large wooden beams, to the majestic, oversized stone fireplace and the expansive deck overlooking the glistening river. I was completely entranced. Not only had I never witnessed such splendor I had not been treated with such special attention in my entire life.

Edward escorted me through the flocked forest to show me his nearby home in the woods. He had built a small log cabin five years before and had lived there ever since. He was the outdoorsy type with two dogs and a rustic lifestyle. Of course, being an extreme nature and dog lover, those pieces added yet another layer of allure. I viewed his life as idyllic. What could possibly be wrong with such a reputable Christian man and his well-respected Christian family who appeared so loving? They were the family I had always longed for.

As we continued on our journey to Montana the day after our stay with Edward and his parents, Viv made her opinion clear. "That was just so incredible! They are such amazing people!" she exclaimed. "How do you feel?"

I pondered her question. "They all seem like wonderful people."

"Do you feel like you could be more than friends with Edward?"

I paused. I still felt hesitancy about moving beyond friendship, even despite the siren song.

"I'm not sure," I stated.

Viv drove home her point. "Well, I think this is a once-in-a-lifetime opportunity. If you pass it up, you'll most likely regret that choice."

Don remained silent as he drove through the snow, while I, sitting in the back seat, felt duly chastened by my big sister. In spite of the quiet voice nudging me toward caution, I returned to the pattern of overriding my feelings in light of Viv's counsel.

The siren song continued to entrance and overpower my young senses. However, there was still one significant obstacle that prevented me from wholeheartedly embracing the golden opportunity. I was seriously committed to my church's belief system and Edward and his parents did not see eye-to-eye with those beliefs. The obstacle of our doctrinal differences needed to be surmounted before I would proceed any further, and I once again found myself in an internal tug-of-war.

For the first half of my childhood, we had attended a Baptist church, but when I was about 10 years old, Mom decided to change to a "spirit-filled, charismatic" church that practiced speaking in tongues and all the "gifts of the spirit." During my teen years, I was the only child in our family attending church with Mom, so I basically became her protégé.

Now that I was considering leaving the charismatic belief system to follow Viv's guidance, I felt a strong inner conflict between pleasing Mom and pleasing Viv, who along with Don embraced the same belief system as Edward's family. Viv had not been indoctrinated in the charismatic beliefs as I had, since she had left home for college shortly after we had changed churches.

Aside from my first quarter of profligate behavior, I had been attending a charismatic church during my college years as well. In layman terms, "spirit-filled" Christians were on a different level of spirituality than "non-spirit-filled" Christians, and Edward and his parents were in the second category.

While they knew the Bible backwards and forwards, they did not believe in speaking in tongues or in any of the "gifts of the spirit." That doctrinal dilemma launched me into a spiritual crisis, and I decided to do some serious soul searching in order to resolve my inner conflict. I read several books recommended to me by Edward about his beliefs and I in turn shared a few books with him, which he read.

I talked to Viv and Don about my struggle. After several months of earnest praying and reading, I decided to convert. Prior to meeting Edward and his parents, I had not been encouraged to explore my beliefs and after studying both sides I felt their perspective was more aligned with Biblical truth. Viv and her husband seemed very pleased, while Mom seemed the opposite.

At the beginning of my senior year of college Edward and I officially crossed the line from friendship to dating. The only part of me that I registered on a conscious level at that time was the smiling Christian woman. I sincerely believed the Bible verse in 2 Corinthians 5 that states, "Therefore, if anyone is in Christ, he is a new creation; the old has gone, the new has come."[6] I believed with all my heart that my "sinful" past was behind me.

As was typical for a college student, I existed on a minimal budget and lived a no-frills lifestyle in a dorm room just big enough for a twin bed, dresser, desk and sink, with a communal bathroom. I worked part-time jobs to earn spending money and to pay for some of my college expenses. Meeting Edward and his parents was the first time I had contemplated what life might be like in a different financial reality.

In September of my senior year, Edward and his parents invited me to accompany them on a trip with Edward's grandfather. I felt honored and accepted their invitation. I rode with Edward in his new Thunderbird while Mac, Marion and his grandfather rode in a luxury Lincoln Town Car. That weekend was magical, my Snow White fantasy in real life. We stayed in hotels nicer than I had ever seen and savored gourmet meals in upscale restaurants, strengthening the siren's trance.

Edward was a perfect gentleman and did not attempt anything physical the entire weekend. I was not used to that kind of respect from a guy, and I was pleasantly surprised. All I had ever known was the opposite, except of course with Jimmy in third grade. Little did I know at that time that Edward was following Mac and Marion's Christian Code of Honor for dating, which he described to me

---

[6] New International Version Bible, 1973

later like a strict game plan. Control. Clear boundaries. No
sex before marriage.

There were distinct phases which provided specific
guidelines for the physical relationship during the periods
of dating and engagement. The boundaries for the dating
phase involved brief hugging and hand holding. Brief kissing was allowed yet not encouraged during the engagement
phase as the ultimate goal for Christian purity required no
kissing before the wedding day.

Since I clearly had not followed the Christian Code of
Honor during my younger years, and since Edward and his
parents were much more knowledgeable about the Bible, I
began wholeheartedly submitting to their code of conduct.
I wanted to live the pure Christian life.

During the idyllic fall weekend, Edward and I talked
about various topics as we rode together in his Thunderbird. We talked about our relationship histories. He had
lived a pure life and at 27 years old, was still a virgin and
had never even experienced a first kiss.

Impressed by his Christian commitment and pure relationship track record, especially compared to my sinful
past, I felt honored to be the woman who had secured his
affection. When I described my relationship history, I had
to confess my sins, which was very difficult. Although I
had not had a physical relationship with a guy for almost
3 years, I still felt the weight of my sin when I told him I
was not a virgin.

Edward was visibly taken aback when he heard of my
impurity and clearly concerned about the fact that I was

no longer a virgin. According to Mac and Marion, marrying a virgin was a high priority. He would be compromising his code of Christian honor if he stayed in a relationship with me. In spite of his misgivings and with such a massive strike against me, Edward decided to keep my sinful past between the two of us, and we continued dating according to their code.

I wanted to prove my deep commitment to living the Christian life and fully agreed to do things their way. I accepted that I was the "inferior" one due to my history of sexual sin. Looking back, my heart breaks as I reflect on how I willingly strapped on the heavy yoke of moral inferiority and followed their lead. Sure, I had made choices that I regretted. I had also learned and changed.

Now when I think of how I allowed shame to pin me into submission, I am deeply saddened. Yet that was how I had been raised. Fornication was a sin. From that point on any difficulties that arose in my relationship with Edward were laid at my feet due to the fact that I had not been a virgin when we married. I was the problem, damaged goods, and the only course for reparation was to obey God, the Bible and Edward. No questions asked.

Edward revealed to me that I was his ideal physical partner in terms of physical attraction. Tall, thin, athletic, long dark hair. Over the months, he and his parents showered me with expensive gifts, the likes of which I had never seen. Extravagant chocolates, exquisite perfume, a diamond pendant necklace. The volume of the siren song increased.

During the fall and winter of my senior year of college, I paid to travel by bus every other weekend to stay with Edward and his parents. They graciously hosted me in their luxurious guest room overlooking the river, complete with private balcony and bathroom, lush carpet and king-sized bed. They fed me delicious food, distinctly unlike my regular college diet. I participated with them in their family Bible reading and prayer time every evening.

They continued treating me like I was so special and loved, which was the holy grail of emotional connection for which I had desperately searched my entire childhood. The feelings I had sought to no avail within my family of origin were showered on me in abundance. They showed a great deal of interest in me and seemed to care deeply about me as a person. They treated me as a cherished member of their family and I in turn cherished every moment of their affection. Like Snow White and the tantalizing apple, I eagerly accepted their offering.

In December I was invited to Edward and Mac's company Christmas party. They were well known in the business community and being invited to their Christmas part felt like an extreme honor for a simple country girl from Montana. Shortly after accepting their generous invitation, I registered the alarming reality that I had nothing to wear to that would be remotely suitable for the grand occasion. I was Cinderella minus a fairy godmother.

I did not own a car at that time, so I journeyed by city bus to the small shopping mall in my college town and to my delight I discovered a store affiliated with Nordstrom. I had learned by then that Edward and his parents shopped almost exclusively at Nordstrom. My delight soon turned to dismay when I looked at the price tags. I could not afford such prices on my minimal college budget. I lived on a cash-only financial plan and did not have the luxury of a credit card.

Fortunately, I managed to find two elegant dresses on the sale rack that seemed suitable for the holiday gala. One was a two-piece, fuchsia sweater dress combination and the other a belted, cream linen one piece. I felt very guilty as I paid for those dresses. That kind of ostentatious spending ran cross-grain to the practical lifestyle of my childhood. I had never spent so much money on clothing in all my days. However, desperate times called for desperate measures.

In January of 1987 Edward wrote a letter to Dad asking for my hand in marriage. Dad and Mom were on a fishing trip in Texas at the time. Although Mom and Dad had only spoken with Edward when he came to their home in June of 1985, Dad responded in the affirmative. Mac and Marion were thrilled. The green light for our engagement had been given. We went shopping for my ring and ultimately chose a sparkling solitaire with an accompanying wedding band set with small diamonds. With all the details in perfect order, our engagement day arrived.

Our engagement took place on Valentine's Day, 1987. Edward and I had discussed marriage for several months prior to the big day, and he planned the engagement in conjunction with Tiffany's counsel. The plan involved a long hike up a snow-covered mountain, one of Edward's favorite activities. He knew I loved nature and assumed I would love an arduous hike in winter conditions as much as he did.

We left for our destination in the morning and drove several hours north to where Mac and Marion owned some land. Although I was thrilled with the reality of being soon engaged to Edward as well as the beauty of the scenery, I became exhausted as we hiked for several hours through deep snow with Edward plowing the trail in front of me. I was in good shape in those days, yet my physical endurance did not come close to matching his.

We reached our destination on the side of the mountain. The blue-sky day was exquisite and the view stunning, as Edward carved out a bench in the side of a deep snowbank. I sat on my wintry loveseat while he dug a fire pit, gathered wood and started a fire. Once the fire was crackling, he dug into his backpack and brought out a small box of two chocolates, one for each of us. After soaking up the fire and view for a while, he pulled the ring from his backpack and sat down on the loveseat next to me. My 21-year-old heart filled with joy as he asked, "Will you marry me?" I enthusiastically responded "Yes!" with a big smile on my face, believing with all my heart that the wonderful prince whom I loved, loved me. Like Snow White, I felt confident we would live happily ever after.

The inner part of me that had tried to convey messages of caution, the part hidden and silenced in the thick fog, had intuited the truth. She had sensed the dangers ahead and yet my entranced Self remained deaf to her warnings.

The volume of the siren song drowned out any thoughts or feelings that did not coincide with my longed-for childhood fantasy. My split Self, two parts with completely different feelings, existed in one body with only one part being seen and heard. Even to myself.

DANGERS UNHEEDED

In March, Mac and Marion hosted an engagement party in an upscale restaurant and invited close family and friends. Mom and Dad chose to stay in Texas and enjoy their time as "snowbirds," fishing near the Gulf of Mexico, as they had done during previous winters since Dad's retirement in 1983. I was disappointed, yet not at all surprised.

Now that I would soon be "family," Mac and Marion suggested I call them Mom and Dad, which I gladly chose to do as I felt privileged to be considered one of their beloved daughters. If they had been privy to my subversive physical interactions with their pure son, they may not have been as enthusiastic about welcoming me. Edward and I had not completely honored the purity code. We had held hands and kissed prior to entering the engagement phase. I take responsibility for crossing the scandalous kissing line. I initiated the forbidden action several months before our engagement during a moment of intense emotion. I was in love.

With our engagement firmly set by the sparkling, one carat diamond solitaire ring, Edward and I entered into pre-marital counseling with Mac and Marion, which I considered an extreme honor. They were revered by many for their exemplary Christian marriage and for counseling numerous other young Christian couples prior to marriage, including their other adult children and their spouses.

During my weekend visits and over the course of several months, Mac and Marion instructed us on many aspects of Christian marriage, especially how the man was the head of the home and the wife was to submit to his authority out of obedience to God. They backed every bit of their counsel with the power of the Bible.

"Wives, submit yourselves to your own husbands as you do to the Lord. For the husband is the head of the wife as Christ is the head of the church, his body, of which he is Savior."[7] (Ephesians 5:22-23) That was not new information. I had been taught by the Bible and by Mom's example. I was already programmed to obey Edward based in fear of God.

The topic I remember discussing the most was "intimacy". I had never openly discussed sex, which had felt like a taboo subject during my childhood. Other than the Bible verses and the notes Mom had left on my dresser, I only knowledge came from my past experiences with Scott, Dillon and Brad, which I had not shared with anyone except with Edward.

---

[7] New International Version Bible, 1973

Instead of treating the topic like a dirty subject, Mac and Marion glorified and expanded on the benefits. They taught us that "intimacy" was a high priority for a godly marriage and for that reason several hours a week needed to be "scheduled", allowing both parties to be emotionally and physically prepared, in contrast to frequent "maintenance" times where less time and energy would be expected. Unbeknownst to my naïve sensibilities, they lined out a plan in which I would ultimately have no choice. They highlighted that men were more interested than women and yet according to the Bible the wife's body belonged not to her, but to her husband. Sex was a "marital duty" to be fulfilled. The following verses made my duty to Edward crystal clear.

"The husband should fulfill his marital duty to his wife, and likewise the wife to her husband. The wife's body does not belong to her alone but also to her husband."[8] (I Corinthians 7:3-4)

My subconscious programming and naïveté, on top of my desire to obey God, produced the result of unquestioning acceptance of their Biblical instruction. Decades later I would fully comprehend that their "counsel" dictated the perfect life for a controlling, sexually addicted husband. I would also come to understand through years of painful experience that their teaching constituted the essence of

---

[8] New International Version Bible, 1973

rape, which I referred to earlier from Diane Langberg's book, *Suffering and the Heart of God*, as occurring when there is the threat of harm.[9] I never once doubted the severe eternal consequences if I disobeyed.

As had been true since my earliest years, my obedience to God remained inextricably linked to the avoidance of punishment and I lived in constant terror of the consequences of disobedience. I absorbed Mac and Marion's counsel and my response was no different. Obedience was my only option, or else. As with my childhood teachings, I now realize their instruction represented nothing less than abuse in the name of God. But at that time, it was all I had ever known.

Our wedding date was set during the summer of 1987. In March I traveled abroad as a part of my studies during my last quarter of college. Several years prior I had arranged for my participation in a foreign exchange program and leaving right after our engagement was very difficult. I had become emotionally attached to Edward and he to me. We tearfully said goodbye at the airport as we felt the extreme emotional deprivation of a three-month separation.

After I finished my schooling in Spain, Edward and his parents traveled to meet me in Europe. Unlike my parents who only traveled to places in the western United States where Dad could hunt or fish, Mac and Marion enjoyed traveling to places unassociated with those hobbies. We spent a magical week at a little hotel in Switzerland, sightseeing and traveling through the Swiss alps. Everywhere

---

[9] Suffering and the Heart of God, 2015

we went and everything we saw took my breath away. The siren trance once again carried me away on the furious current of euphoria.

The only emotional speed bump occurred when I informed Edward that I had partaken of two beers on separate occasions during my stay with my Spanish host family. I told him I had been exhausted and stressed by the loud, late night conversations in their home and, as a last resort, drank the beers to help me sleep.

Upon hearing of my choices, Edward immediately became silent and emotionally distant, which was the first time I had felt that energy from him. His body stiffened and his face grew serious. In an instant I felt the all too familiar stab of panic from deep within and my nervous system kicked into high alert. Finally, he spoke.

"Drinking is not allowed in my family. My uncle died of alcoholism. One night when he was drunk, he fell asleep in my parent's garage with the car still running. My dad found him dead the next morning."

Edward's emotional response to the traumatic memory of his uncle's death manifested in anger, triggering my old subconscious survival mechanism. I instinctively scrambled to create a feeling of safety for myself through appeasing him. Although I apologized profusely for my error in judgment and promised I would never drink again, I felt his anger for several days afterward, which manifested in the same painful manner I had experienced with Dad and Brad when I displeased them. Emotional withdrawal and punishing silence.

I once again took the position of inferiority while explaining I had been given many opportunities to drink and party, especially since the father of my host family was a liquor distributor for numerous nightclubs in the region. In fact, he had frequently extended the invitation for me to experience the culture and night life. By my own choice I declined his invitations.

Edward's angry, guilt-tripping reaction to my adult choice of having a few beers should have sent off giant red flares in my mind, especially as the shame-game escalated. The healthy, freedom-based choice would have been to put on my running shoes and do an imitation of Julia Roberts as the runaway bride. Unfortunately, I was sunk too deep in fear and my pattern of submitting to an angry man to understand there was a healthier way to live.

The scenario with the two beers was not the first time I had glimpsed the reality of Edward's anger. During our engagement he had shared a story which should have raised grave concerns. However, as we were soon to be married, I dismissed any concerns because he loved me, and I loved him.

The story he shared had taken place when he was 18 years old. The setting was the Baptist family camp located across the river from his parents' home. As was common, Marion was "sick" in bed one night. Across the river a group of children and camp counselors were singing around a campfire near the water's edge. Marion became upset due to the fact that the noise prevented her from sleeping. She complained to Mac who then shared her distress with Edward. When Edward learned of how the campers were upsetting his mother, he became enraged. Unknown to his parents, Edward grabbed his rifle and silently rowed across the river in his canoe. With rifle in hand, he stepped onto the shore and approached the happy children and camp counselors in the darkness, holding them at gunpoint. He demanded they stop singing. The children and counselors froze, wide-eyed and terrified. One of the counselors talked to Edward, managing to calm him down enough to surrender the gun. The police were called, and Edward was taken to the police station. Mac and Marion received a phone call notifying them of their son's actions. Upon arriving at the police station, they convinced the officers to release Edward with only a warning. After that day the event was not spoken of again.

As I listened to Edward's story of rage and how he not only terrified but threatened to kill innocent children and camp counselors, I was offered insight into his emotional life. But even with that opportunity to consider his disclosure and the potential implications for our relationship, I never reconsidered my future with Edward.

Soon after our return from Switzerland, Edward, Mac and Marion traveled to my college graduation ceremony, as did Mom and Dad. I joined my graduating classmates and was seated in the center of the large gymnasium, the audience surrounding in the bleachers. I waved at Edward, his parents and my parents now and then during the ceremony.

I was seated next to a male classmate and friend, and

we talked and laughed quietly a few times. After the ceremony was over, Edward shared a comment that Mac had made while he observed me talking to my classmate. "You will need to keep a close eye on that one and make sure you maintain control."

Again, such a dictatorial comment should have set off alarm bells and caused me to seriously consider the repercussions of male dominance. However, in keeping with my view of submission, I accepted Mac's statement as a confirmation of my position. I would soon be Edward's wife and I needed to submit to his authority. Although I had no idea what my future self would be required to do to make that happen, my eager young self was determined to prove my devotion to him and God. Snow White was determined to ride off with her prince and live happily ever after.

One way I proved my submissive attitude was through giving Edward and his parents control over my future career. Prior to graduation, Edward and I had discussed the possibility of my getting a job after we married. I had graduated with honors and a bachelor's degree in Business Management. Edward had spoken to one of his banking contacts who was willing to consider me for the position of loan officer.

Having been a bank teller during my summer breaks from college, I was familiar with banking and felt excited about the possibility. When Edward mentioned my potential career to Mac and Marion, they persuaded him that the wiser plan would be for me to forego getting a full-time job for the purpose of keeping my schedule flexible, enabling me to travel with them or adjust to their schedules whenever necessary.

During our weekly Friday night dinner in a restaurant, Mac explained to me, "We want to have the freedom to travel and be together whenever possible. Since Edward and I have control over our schedules, your flexibility will give us the freedom to do what we want, when we want." Rather than registering the danger of handing over control of my future, I wanted to please them and once again chose to submit to their counsel.

The wedding weekend arrived in the summer of 1987, just a week after my 22nd birthday. I awoke to a beautiful morning in Mac and Marion's luxurious guest room with the glorious anticipation of starting a perfect life with my prince whom I loved. I arrived at the small community church in order to ready myself for the late morning photo session before the afternoon ceremony.

I styled my hair, applied my makeup, and changed into my wedding dress in the church's small restroom. Eerily, I wore Mom's wedding dress and veil, as Viv had done before me. At that time my choice of dress was a given. I had not for one moment considered wearing anything else. I am haunted as I remember that detail, a prophetic omen.

Viv and Tiffany, the two matchmakers responsible for our union, stood as the matron of honor and bridesmaid. Edward's older brother, Sam, and his best friend, Tom, served as best man and groomsman. I had asked Ted and Seth to fill the role of ushers and they had agreed, a decision which I would live to regret.

After the scheduled time for the photo session, Ted and Seth meandered in late wearing tank tops and shorts, with fast food beverages and tuxedos in hand. They acted completely nonchalant, as if their late arrival did not matter at all. The truth was I did not matter to them, and I never had. My wedding day was just one time of many when they took the opportunity to communicate their feelings to me.

Our wedding ceremony played out in front of approximately 150 guests who filled the pews. Beautifully decorated with pink, red and cream-colored flowers, the small church sanctuary resembled an adorned rustic lodge, with a rich wood interior and an A-frame vaulted ceiling.

The wedding party was dressed in dark rose-colored dresses and grey tuxedos, with Edward's tuxedo white to match my dress. The ceremony was traditional Christian with a few added twists for spiritual impact.

Dad escorted me down the aisle to the sound of the customary processional music. Mac preached a mini sermon. The pastor of the church preached a mini sermon aimed at converting the guests to Jesus. Viv and her husband sang two Christian songs.

At the end of the hour-long ceremony, I turned to face our guests with a brilliant smile on my face. I was overjoyed as I walked down the aisle with my prince as *Mr. and Mrs.* We lined up along with our parents and wedding members to greet our guests.

The next step in my married journey unfolded as Edward's older brother and best man, Sam, "chauffeured" us from the church to the reception. His approach to creating joy for us on our wedding day involved driving recklessly, speeding down neighborhood streets around blind corners, laughing all the way. While I was genuinely afraid, Edward laughed right along with him, not seeming to notice my discomfort.

The wedding reception was held outside at the same beautiful, high rise hotel on the lake where I had been awestruck a few years prior while having dinner with Edward. The weather was picture perfect. The guests enjoyed the beautiful outdoor setting by the shimmering lake, the delicious food and beverages, and the cake.

Other than a minor mishap with the cake, the day played out ideally. When evening approached, I felt both very tired and very happy. I was thrilled to be Edward's wife and emotionally and physically drained by the events of the day. I entered my honeymoon night with the anticipation of physical intimacy with Edward and much needed rest.

Our wedding night was scheduled at the same highrise hotel. The room and view were breathtaking, overlooking the lake. As counseled by Mac and Marion, I had prepared myself by purchasing a gorgeous negligee. To ensure that my choice would please Edward, I even went so far as to model my sheer outfit for Marion. She bestowed her approval on my choice, and I felt confident that Edward would be pleased.

A few weeks prior to the wedding Mom had offered me one succinct piece of advice for my marriage. "When it comes to sex, men want it a lot more than women." That was the extent of marriage counseling from my parents. Until my wedding night, I believed my future would be perfect with my prince. In reality, the only difference between my past and my future was the fact that my future was permanent. I had been able to leave my childhood home. I was also able to get away from Brad. But as a married woman, I now had the lifelong Christian duty of submitting to Edward, until death do us part. In my mind, divorce would never be an option. The Bible clearly prohibited divorce, except under the conditions of adultery.

"To the married I give this command (not I, but the Lord): A wife must not separate from her husband".[1011] (I Corinthians 7:10)

"'For I hate divorce,' says the Lord, the God of Israel".

During the months before my wedding, I bypassed several opportunities to take a step back and seriously consider the dangers hidden beneath the idyllic surface. Instead, the siren song drowned out the wakeup calls offered to me. With the words, "I do," I unknowingly walked into a prison of trauma.

---

[10] New International Bible, 1973

[11] New International Bible, 1973

THE PRISON OF TRAUMA

I had looked forward to our honeymoon night, antici-
pating a different physical reality with Edward than
I had previously experienced. I had not had a physical
relationship for almost four years and believed my painful
experiences were long gone. I believed incorrectly.

My wedding night was the first time I intuitively sensed
that Edward and Brad had the same addictive sexual energy. What I did not know during my engagement period that
I eventually learned from Edward after we were married
was the fact that his older brother had taught him to mas-
turbate when Edward was 11 years old. Since then, he had
frequently engaged in that emotional coping mechanism.

My perception of Edward as a virgin was true only in so
far as he had never experienced intercourse. That fact did not
diminish his addiction to the powerful chemical effects. He
had become addicted to the "fix" long before he met me. Now
that he had a dutiful Christian wife whose body belonged to
him, he no longer had to get his fix through his own efforts.

After having sex with Edward for the first time on our wedding night, I succumbed to sheer exhaustion. Not long after I had fallen asleep, I was awakened when he initiated again. I submitted. Again. That cycle repeated a few more times during the night, in spite of my exhaustion. I truly believed that I had no choice but to surrender my body to him out of obedience to God.

I do not know how or when I registered the truth that night. All I know is that at some point I became aware on a deep level that Edward's sexual energy replicated Brad's. The pressure, the drive, the lack of consideration for my feelings. This striking epiphany swept over me in an instant. As I submitted my body to him the awareness that I was trapped engulfed me like a tsunami. I truly believed I had no voice and no choice. For me, that truth equated to life as a sex slave.

In a moment my inner world shifted, like tectonic plates being moved by an unstoppable force, creating an entirely different landscape. I was no longer the delighted bride in a luxury honeymoon suite with her prince. Although there were no exterior indications revealing my change, I felt like a prisoner locked in a prison cell, with Edward and God as my jailers.

As had happened involuntarily many times during my young years and with Brad when I could not cope with my emotions, I dissociated. The real "me," the part of me who felt the truth, detached and retreated into the thick dark fog, silenced. I could not bear the feelings of entrapment and terror. I had to do whatever was necessary to survive.

I began the second day of my honeymoon as a different woman. Although I was completely exhausted, the smiling Christian woman was fully visible, playing the role of performer, and the part of me who knew the truth retreated into darkness and silence. That part of me could not be given a voice in my new life. She did not meld with my goal of being a submissive Christian wife.

Although I have no memories of that second day, I know we flew to the Virgin Islands for a week at a resort on St. Croix. I remember only a few snapshots of that Caribbean setting. Bath temperature blue water. The sound of steel drums.

We had scheduled the second week of our honeymoon in Aspen, Colorado. We arrived in Denver late at night and rented a car for the four-hour drive to Aspen. The only memories I have of the second week occurred during that night and the next morning. Edward stopped at a gas station in the middle of the night. As he pulled up to the gas pumps, large clouds of moths swarmed around the overhead lights. I stayed in the car while Edward got out to pump gas and buy beverages and snacks. Each time he opened the car door, large moths flew inside.

As we departed the gas station, the large moths with their gripping legs landed on my bare arms and legs. In spite of the total darkness, I tried to fend them off as best I could. In the process of trying to protect myself from the barrage, I spilled soda from the open can in my hand, eliciting Edward's anger.

"Stop waving your arms around! You're spilling soda

all over the car!"

My nervous system immediately registered his anger, and I instinctively froze. I do not remember anything else about the drive except fending off moths and trying to sleep to no avail while Edward sang Christian songs loudly with his window rolled down for the purpose of staying awake. We arrived in Aspen in the early hours of the morning. The next thing I knew Edward climbed out of bed and got dressed at six a.m.

"Where are you going?" I asked in my half-awake state.

With a curt tone, he stated, "I'm going to the car wash to clean the soda and moths out of the car, so I don't get charged a cleaning fee."

As I laid alone in bed, I felt the deep pain of emotional disconnection and the reality that saving money on a rental car cleaning deposit was more important to my new husband than being with me. Just like with Dad, Ted, and Brad, I felt Edward's punishing anger acutely. That is the last memory I have of the second week of my honeymoon.

Two weeks after my wedding day I returned home in a state of dissociation, unknown to anyone, even myself. As if on autopilot, I defaulted to my survival instinct. Smile, obey and make people happy. The routines that became a part of my autopilot life when we returned from our honeymoon included weekly scheduled and daily maintenance sex; accomplishing my household duties such as cooking, cleaning and buying groceries; revolving around Edward and his parents; and, of course, going to church once or twice a week. I cheerfully and obediently fulfilled my duties to God and Edward.

In my free time I frequented the local gym, an activity which was fully supported by Edward due to the fact that he militantly pursued daily physical exercise to maintain a perfect physique. I attended aerobics classes and became acquainted with several of the women instructors, who encouraged me to attend a training seminar to become certified as an aerobics instructor. I thought that sounded like fun so with Edward's approval, I earned my certification. I taught a few classes at the gym each week and my part-time employment allowed me enough flexibility to revolve my life around Edward and his parents.

Another job that had always sounded interesting to me was modeling, which was not surprising considering my teenage desire to look and feel pretty. Again, that was flexible, part-time employment and Edward approved. I could accept whatever jobs I wanted and reject those that conflicted with him or his parents.

There was a reputable modeling agency nearby and I signed a contract to model for them. Before long I had landed a few small jobs such as the glamorous career launcher of starring as a foot model in a commercial for a podiatrist. Over time I was also hired for several runway shows for higher-end department stores.

Although I earned a little income from these various jobs, Edward was in control of the money and if I wanted to purchase something I had to ask his permission. I wanted spending money of my own, so I tried to think creatively about other flexible part-time jobs. I spoke with Edward about any possibilities, and he in turn spoke with Mac. Together they created what they deemed a suitable job position and magnanimously offered me the job of garbage collector. My job responsibilities entailed picking up trash in the parking lots of their local commercial real estate buildings. They rewarded my labor with $25 per parking lot. The fact that I did not even think how demeaning their job offer was or about the fact that as a woman with a bachelor's degree I was capable of so much more reveals how thoroughly programmed I was to submit to male authority without question.

One year after our wedding we moved out of our executive home and purchased a fixer upper closer to Mac and Marion, affording us the ability to walk a short distance through the forest to Edward's log cabin and Mac and Marion's house. Edward saw our home as a long-term investment, and we worked together to improve it. I painted the entire exterior while Edward did miscellaneous repairs and built a deck on the front. I faithfully continued my regular wifely duties which per usual involved grocery shopping.

There were several groceries stores in the area that I frequented to find the best prices. Edward typically asked about the cost of the groceries and often asked for the receipt after each shopping trip. If I overspent, I was subjected to punishing silence, therefore I made every effort to find the best deals. One of the grocery stores where I shopped employed an assistant manager named Keith who usually greeted me with a friendly smile and hello.

Over the course of about six months, Keith and I became better acquainted during my shopping trips. At one point we discussed where we lived and discovered we only lived a few blocks from each other. Another day, we discovered we exercised at the same gym. Although I did not consciously register my feelings of attraction, I felt something when I was with Keith that I did not feel with Edward. Emotional connection and kindness. My emotionally starved Self responded to my instinctive need and I felt drawn toward Keith, like a moth to the flame.

One evening Edward went camping overnight and I went for a walk around the neighborhood with our dog. I decided to stop by Keith's house to say hello. We talked for a few hours and crossed the line from friends to more than friends. For the next month, we spent time together when possible. Although I felt emotional connection with Keith that I did not feel with Edward, I also felt intensely guilty.

The only way I knew to resolve my extreme inner conflict was to return to my childhood template of obedience to God. I prayed fervently, asking God for forgiveness. In my mind, divorce was not an option. In spite of my feelings for Keith, I confessed my infidelity to Edward and told Keith I could not see him anymore.

Regretting my unfaithfulness deeply, I apologized to Edward many times. He chose to stay in our marriage, and we decided not to tell anyone about my affair. We had sex the night after I confessed. He did not skip a beat in that regard. He had told me several times during our marriage that sex was his *only* joy in life. In the middle of his distress, he beelined to his favorite coping mechanism, his real joy, and I was the sole source of his supply.

Every day I felt the weight of my guilt and wanted to ensure I never crossed the line of infidelity again. With Edward's permission, I told Viv about my affair for the purpose of her holding me accountable to my marriage vow. She was basically my fidelity parole officer. I voluntarily checked in with her and Edward frequently to report my activities. I willingly submitted to my repentance requirements.

To safeguard against future infidelity, I memorized Bible verses specifically pertaining to faithfulness in marriage and recited them often. I voluntarily discontinued teaching aerobics and modeling to ensure protection against any future temptations. I stopped shopping at the grocery store where Keith worked. Whenever I was in public, I did not make eye contact with men.

A few months later, in December of 1989, I found out I was pregnant. I was thrilled with the news and very excited about the future. Although I did not feel enjoyment in most of my life, I loved being pregnant and preparing for the arrival of our baby. I felt so much joy when I thought of the day when he or she would arrive. I decorated the room and sat in the rocking chair thinking about when I would be holding him or her, or about when he or she would be sleeping in the crib. I spent hours just sitting in the room envisioning my new life as a mother.

In August of 1990 our beautiful baby boy, Larson (Lars), was born. Weighing in at ten pounds, two ounces, he was a very healthy baby. When I saw him, I felt overwhelming love like I had never felt before in my life. He was so perfect and miraculous. The closest feeling that I had experienced in the past was my emotional connection with my dogs. The love I felt for Lars was like the purest, brightest ray of light, penetrating through the thick dark fog into the deepest place of my heart. He was a precious gift and I cherished him. That day was the beginning of my incredible journey as a mother and discovering the true meaning of love. From that moment on, I had a new overriding purpose and powerful heart desire. My goal was to be the best mom I could be to give Lars all the love and caring he deserved.

Soon after Lars' birth I began to understand how caring for his needs and pleasing Edward would be conflicting interests. Edward was like another child competing for my time, attention, and my body. He resented the fact that I wore a nursing bra to bed. As had been true since our honeymoon, he wanted me to sleep naked so he could have full access to my body whenever he wanted.

Although he supported my choice to breastfeed, he did not like the fact that he had to share my breasts, even with a baby. He viewed my body as his property and from his perspective he no longer had sole ownership. I dared to a wear a nursing bra and pads simply because I needed the support for my breasts which were often uncomfortable and leaking.

Another aspect of Edward's control that shifted out of necessity after childbirth was my availability for intercourse. The doctor gave us the mandate that there was to be no intercourse for a minimum of six weeks. Lars' delivery had been difficult, and I had stitches that needed to heal. Edward eagerly counted down the days as the six weeks passed, and I obediently submitted to him once the mandatory waiting period was over.

During the period of time when intercourse was prohibited and subsequently after the birth of each of my babies, Edward required me to fulfill my conjugal duty manually. As my Christian husband, servicing himself was out of the question. I was his wife, and his satisfaction was my sole responsibility.

At bedtime Edward would squeeze K-Y jelly into my open palm, and I would do my duty. At times the job took longer, and the supply of K-Y had to be replenished. Sometimes the job required switching hands due to fatigue. I never questioned his authority. I just submitted to doing my duty.

Child discipline also became an issue when Lars was young. Edward had been raised with strict Biblical discipline that did not allow for a child to misbehave or disobey. Mac and Marion lived by the Bible verse, "Spare the rod, spoil the child."[12] (Proverbs 13:24) Any overt or perceived disobedience was punished. Mac and Marion had instilled their parenting and discipline philosophies in Edward who aimed to obediently follow their example. Throughout his childhood, Edward had been spanked with a belt and at times whipped with jumper cables for disobedience. Their

---

[12] New International Version Bible, 1973

belief was that the child began trying to control the parent from the beginning and therefore the parent had to communicate to the child, no matter how young, that he or she was not in control. Lars was a quiet, sensitive child and required very little discipline. When he became mobile and started exploring his world, he did what every curious little one does by touching everything and anything. If Lars did something that displeased Edward, such as touching something that was off limits, Edward reprimanded him with a loud, stern "NO." Most times Lars cried and obeyed immediately at the mere sound of Edward's command. At times he was disciplined with a slap to the hand.

At a young age, Lars became afraid of Edward. One day when he was around two years old, he was standing in the living room near the door leading out to the garage when Edward returned home from work. The moment Edward walked through the door Lars fell to the floor, crying. That was not the response of a child who felt happy when his daddy came home, but rather the spontaneous act of a child who became afraid at the sight of his father.

As a young mother I carried on as the submissive Christian wife. In spite of having a young baby, I continued to submit to Edward's requirements. If I hinted at being too tired or not feeling well, he emphasized my "promise" to fulfill my duty. Resistance was futile. With that brief reminder, I quickly surrendered.

My prison life provided no emotional rewards except the pure joy of being Lars' mother. Unquestioning obedience to God and Edward was my life. Every Sunday I dressed up, put on a smile, and stood by Edward's side at church morning and evening. I did not once consider changing my situation. I had no awareness that I had that option.

DARK NIGHT OF THE SOUL

Six years prior, in the fall of 1985, while I was a college student in Oregon, Edward had traveled to visit his sister Tiffany and her family. He also came to visit me and took me to dinner at a quaint Bavarian restaurant. Somehow our discussion that night evolved into the topic of having children one day and how many children we would each like to have.

Edward was the youngest of five children and I was the youngest of four. We both stated that we wanted our futures to involve children and came to the conclusion that each of us would like to have four. Prior to that day, I had not consciously thought about if or when I would like to have children. Looking back, I can see no other reason why, at the age of 20, I would have committed myself to such a long-term plan other than the fact that my childhood programming made my decision for me.

Mom was my role model and she had four children. If I were to follow in her exemplary footsteps, that would be my Christian path as well. Aside from the fact that I blindly followed Mom's example, I am and always have been beyond grateful to the Universe for guiding me to have four children. They have by far been the greatest blessings and healers in my life.

After Lars was born, Edward and I decided we wanted to have our first two children close together in age and our beautiful Sara was born 18 months after Lars in late February of 1992. When I first caught sight of her, I was head over heels in love again. My emotional connection with her was just as strong as with Lars, shining a pure, bright light, piercing through my inner darkness. She joined Lars in the deepest place in my heart. Contrary to Lars being blonde, Sara was born with a full head of dark hair. At nine pounds, she was very healthy and another perfect, miraculous gift.

When Lars was almost three, we began considering moving to a larger home to provide more space for our growing family. Due to the fact that Mac and Marion preferred we live near them, we again searched for a home in their vicinity. After our search proved futile, we decided to build a home on part of the land owned by Mac and Marion.

Construction began in the spring of 1993, involving extensive clearing of pine trees and blasting of rock to clear the homesite and create space for a basement. In June we sold our current home and moved into a 900-square foot rental home in a nearby neighborhood while our future home was under construction. Sara and Lars occupied the two small bedrooms while Edward and I slept in a bed in the living room. Our daily routine for the next five months was visiting the construction site every day to check on progress.

During that busy summer, we decided we wanted our next child to be born two years after Sara which would have been February of 1994. Rather than becoming pregnant quickly as had been the case with Lars and Sara, four months went by before I tested positive. Eventually, around the time we moved into our new home in November, I found out I was pregnant. Lars and Sara were three and almost two. I felt very happy about the new baby and intensely exhausted all at the same time.

Our new home was beautiful with views of the surrounding forest. I felt deeply grateful to be in such a natural, serene setting. Although nothing had changed in terms of my emotional reality with Edward, I truly loved our new living space. The change felt like a breath of new life. As had been true in my childhood, nature always brought me great joy and comfort. Our long driveway was connected to Mac and Marion's, and Edward and Mac commuted to work together every day. All in all, I felt happy being in our new home and pregnant with our third child.

My positive feelings soon shifted when I started bleeding in early January. I was put on bed rest, where I waited and prayed for the baby to live. The bleeding continued for several days. I had not experienced a miscarriage and did not know what to expect. I did, however, know what labor pains felt like and I started having contractions similar to the beginning of labor.

A visit to my obstetrician confirmed the truth. I had suffered a miscarriage. As so many women have experienced, I had already became emotionally attached to my baby and I went into a period of mourning. Marion helped care for Lars and Sara for a few days. I called Mom and told her the news. The only thing I remember about that conversation was her telling me she was sorry. Per usual, I detached from the pain and allowed myself no time for grief. The performer pulled herself together and carried on with her responsibilities. She had no choice. The show had to go on.

I became pregnant again soon after the miscarriage with the due date estimated at early November 1994. During those months of pregnancy, I felt grateful to be carrying our third child and Lars and Sara were the joy of my life. I carried on with fulfilling my duties to Edward and to God, in spite of my continual exhaustion.

Our next precious baby decided to finally make her appearance 11 days after the due date. Beautiful, perfect Violet was another healthy baby girl, weighing ten pounds like her big brother with a head of dark hair like her big sister. As before, my heart overflowed with love and gratitude for our miraculous gift. Just as Lars and Sara had done before her, Violet shone a pure, bright light through my darkness and joined them in the deepest place in my heart. I was thrilled to be her Mama along with them.

Around the time that Lars and Sara were four and two years old, we gathered every night in the living room for family Bible time and singing. As had been true for Edward when he was a child, Lars and Sara were expected to sit quietly and listen. In keeping with Mac and Marion's philosophy of child discipline, any acting out or rebellion against that expectation brought punishment.

Lars had a mellow personality and in general was not as active or energetic as Sara. As would have been true for most little ones at only two years old, Sara had a hard time being quiet and sitting still. One particular evening during family singing and Bible reading time, Sara was distracted and did not sit still and sing as Edward expected.

"Sara, I want you to sit still and sing," he commanded her.

His angry tone scared her, and she started crying.

"Sara, I want you to stop crying and sing. If you don't sit still and sing, I will spank you."

Sara tried with all her might to control herself and stop crying, yet she was so afraid of Edward that her crying only intensified. One of my deepest and most painful regrets as a mother is that I did not stop Edward at that point. He picked her up and took her from the living room to spank her. I was still so thoroughly controlled by my programming as a submissive Christian wife that I watched silently as he took my precious little girl. I sat frozen with Lars as I listened to her screams.

During another night the same scenario played out. In spite of her heroic efforts to not cry, Sara was so afraid of being spanked by Edward that she started crying. Edward viewed her crying as rebellion and commanded her to stop. Again, she was so terrified of him that she could not stop crying. *Edward took her from the room again and spanked her. After the second time, I confronted Edward.*

I stood in the kitchen facing him and stated with conviction, "Sara is not rebelling. She is crying because she is afraid of you and terrified of being spanked. She is too young to control herself. "

Edward looked at me with a serious face and stated, "I don't agree. I think she knows exactly what she is doing."

Edward believed that girls and women only cried for the purpose of manipulating men, even as young as Sara. He and I existed on opposite ends of the emotional continuum about that issue. The next day Edward did what he often did when making a decision. He consulted Mac for advice. Although Mac counseled him to continue spanking Sara when she "rebelled," I did not back down, and the scenario did not happen again.

I was completely devoted to Lars, Sara and Violet, although I know there were many days when I was so tired, overwhelmed and stressed that I could not give them my best. Edward helped with some of the physical responsibilities such as changing diapers, bath and play time, yet I was fully responsible for the emotional nurturing. They were afraid of Edward's anger and in general preferred being with me. I carried the majority of the physical and emotional responsibilities as well as frequently performing my sexual duties. I lived with tunnel vision in the thick, dark, fog, with my children being my only source of light.

In keeping with our conversation more than 10 years prior, our fourth beautiful, perfect baby was born in April of 1997. At nine and a half pounds, Jasmine was another healthy baby girl with blonde hair like her big brother. As with Lars, Sara and Violet, she shone a pure, bright light into my inner darkness and took her place alongside them in the deepest place in my heart. She was another miraculous, precious gift and I was thrilled to be the Mama of four.

Due to the fact that our insurance only allowed one night in the hospital after Jasmine's birth, I booked a hotel room for one night with hopes of getting sleep and being more rested before returning home to our other young children. Like many newborns, Jasmine cried during most of the night in spite of my frequent attempts to nurse her. I drifted in and out of sleep while she alternated between sleeping and crying. From then on sleep became a very elusive goal, which was not surprising considering the continual emotional and physical needs of four young children and a husband who was just as dependent on me as they were.

Along with sex, another source of significant emotional pressure inherent in my relationship with Edward stemmed from his frequent panic attacks. When we were dating, he told me about his panic attacks which had begun during childhood and had continued in his adult life. His attacks were rooted in fear of abandonment, specifically by his parents. Beginning in kindergarten they had occurred when he was separated from Mac and Marion for longer periods of time. Edward had sought therapy different times without significant improvement. When I entered the picture as a young college woman in her early 20's, he had already experienced a long history of panic attacks.

Mac and Marion's Christian philosophy regarding any kind of chronic suffering was based on a portion of the Bible from II Corinthians Chapter 12 where the Apostle Paul wrote that he had a "thorn in the flesh" which he asked God three times to remove from him. God's reply was, "My grace is sufficient for you, for my power is perfected in weakness." Paul then adjusted his attitude accordingly with the following faith-based declaration, "Therefore I will boast all the more gladly in my suffering so that Christ's power may rest of me."[13]

According to this scripture, suffering was an opportunity to experience and demonstrate Christ's power. A badge of honor if you will. A Bible verse was a convenient and noble way to cover the truth – that something insidious was at the root of Edward's panic.

When I first learned of Edward's panic attacks, I felt sorry for him and believed I could help him. Once again, my naïveté prevented me from comprehending the depth of his dark reality. The severe panic attacks he had experienced when his parents went away were transferred to me when we married. I took Mac and Marion's place as his emotional security blanket and he panicked whenever I left for longer periods of time. He always made his panic known to me prior to my departure and I felt guilty leaving him.

I dealt with that suffocating reality for most of our marriage and felt the same level of emotional responsibility for

---

[13] New International Version Bible, 1973

Edward as I did for our four children. He hated whenever I left him alone with the children. I basically cared for five children, with one of them being sexually demanding and controlling.

By the time we had been married for 10 years, I had not been away from Edward for more than a few weekends a year. Although Mac and Marion typically watched the children for one weekend a year so Edward and I could go away together, those trips were not a vacation for me. Edward's expectations for sex were higher than ever when we were alone.

Besides the pressure of Edward's panic whenever I left, our kids did not like when I went away, so I rarely left them for more than a few hours at a time. During one particular instance when Jasmine was little, while I was away for one of my two annual weekend trips, she would not allow Edward to feed her. Sara, being six or seven years old at the time, stepped in and competently took over the feeding. Jasmine happily cooperated with her.

When I did leave, I spent one weekend with Vivian and one weekend visiting my parents. During that period of time Dad was a patient at the state mental hospital in Montana, where he had been admitted in 1994 due to severe dementia. Those visits were not relaxing. Dad had started experiencing signs of early Alzheimer's disease in 1992 at the age of 62. Mom had cared for him at home until his dementia progressed to a point where she could no longer safely care for him.

Although Dad's mental capabilities deteriorated, his

physical strength remained formidable. Several times he escaped and ran away when he lived at home, and Mom would have to enlist help to bring him back. Mom also became more concerned about his temper and potential for violence as his dementia increased. He had far less ability to regulate his emotions and his anger became more uncontrolled. She had resorted to hiding anything that he could use to harm himself or others, such as guns and knives.

One night after she had gone to sleep, Mom heard loud crashing sounds coming from the kitchen. Dad was throwing all the contents of the cupboards and drawers on the floor in search of knives. Broken glasses, dishes and silverware covered the floor. Feeling she was in danger Mom ran to the neighbor's house to call the police who arrived and escorted Dad to a nursing home. He never returned home after that traumatic night. He stayed at the nursing home for a few weeks until the staff determined they could not legally sedate him enough to ensure his safety and the safety of others.

In 1994 Dad was transferred to the Montana State Mental Hospital, a psychiatric facility where he lived until he passed away on Christmas Eve, 1998. During those four years he did not know my name or seemingly recognize me, except for one occasion when I visited in October of 1994. On that day he reacted with a big smile when he saw me. At times he would be unresponsive and other times he would become angry and violent when I arrived, and I would have to leave before the visit even started. Due to the fact that he attacked several patients and staff members, he was constantly strapped in a geriatric chair to ensure he did not harm anyone. Regardless of his age, his pattern of unpredictable anger and volatility never changed.

Although I knew Dad's dementia was the main cause of his behavior, I still felt and saw the same man I had lived with during my childhood. When he passed away, part of me felt grief knowing that I would never have the emotional connection with him for which I had longed my entire life, yet a larger part felt relief knowing that I would never again be subjected to his anger.

I spent one weekend a year with Viv and Edward reluctantly approved. After I had planned my trip several months in advance, he dreaded my departure, and I felt the weight of his anxiety as the trip approached. The children also became anxious before I left, and I felt the weight of my responsibility for them.

One weekend I had spent a few days with Viv at a Christian women's retreat in a serene, natural setting. At the end of the final session on Sunday morning, when the speaker was making her final remarks, she casually referred to returning home to our regular lives and how we would benefit by remembering and applying our learned inspiration.

Despite the fact that she intended to boost our mental and emotional strength, her words had the opposite effect on me. Out of nowhere I was hit by a tsunami of emotions. Before I knew what was happening, I was weeping uncontrollably.

Years later when I looked back on that day, I realized

that the speaker's reference to going back to my prison with Edward filled my heart with overwhelming dread. Just the thought of returning to the crushing weight of responsibility and obligation triggered a tidal wave of emotion. I pulled myself together and returned home to fulfill my duties as a submissive Christian wife. I did not breathe a word about my breakdown to anyone, and Viv asked very few questions. She viewed me as having the perfect life. She had no idea what my regular schedule entailed.

My scheduled "intimacy" time with Edward typically occurred on Saturday afternoons. I had agreed to that time as that was usually the least stressful day of the week. I was expected to wear a sexy outfit, show enthusiasm and experience an orgasm (which I faked most times due to lack of desire and exhaustion). In contrast, the daily "maintenance" times occurred before we went to sleep every night and only required that I passively participate long enough for him to procure his fix.

On one particular Saturday morning I did not feel well enough to perform and asked for a reprieve from our scheduled session. As I stood next to the sink in our master bathroom, I told Edward with trepidation, "I feel like I'm coming down with a stomach bug. Can we wait until next weekend?"

His stoic expression offered no empathy or sign of compassion. After a few seconds of staring at me in silence he responded, "But you promised, and I've been looking forward to this all week" meaning I had agreed on Saturday afternoons. In a few brief seconds I once again registered his telltale lack of empathy and resigned myself to obedience.

In May of 1998, when Jasmine was one year old, Mac and Marion gave Edward and me the "gift" of a ten-year anniversary vacation. Truthfully, I did not feel comfortable leaving my young children with them for a week. However, Mac and Marion had given the same gift to their other four children and their spouses, and they strongly encouraged us to go. Their gift included a one-week, all-expenses paid vacation to the destination of our choice.

Despite my reluctance to leave the kids and be alone with Edward for that long, I accepted their gift and thanked them for their kindness. We planned a cruise through the Inside Passage to Alaska. On the morning of our departure, 6-year-old Sara woke up with a fever. I kissed her goodbye as she lay on the couch. With tears filling her eyes, she cried, "Please don't go Mommy". My heart broke. I did not want to leave, but I forced myself to turn around and walk out the door.

Mac and Marion had instructed us that we were not to be in contact with them and the kids during our trip unless there was an emergency. Likewise, they would not contact us unless there was an emergency. Their mandate was given so that we could enjoy our romantic vacation together. Although I chafed against their instruction, I submitted to their authority.

My limited memories of that trip are the stunning Alaskan scenery, being preoccupied with thoughts of my children, being seasick and performing. I am very prone to motion sickness and during one night of the cruise the ship had to sail out into the open ocean for the purpose of avoiding shallow water in the Inside Passage. We had just finished dinner and were sitting in the ship's theatre waiting for the show to start when in an instant the giant vessel rose up on a large wave and came crashing down. My stomach lurched up and down with the wave and a few seconds later I bolted for our cabin, barely arriving in time for my dinner to exit my body.

Due to the fact that I had to stay next to the toilet, Edward obtained two motion sickness pills from the concierge. When he handed them to me, I did not even question if I should take one or two. Two seemed like the only logical choice. After a few days I became coherent again and the ship's concierge informed me that due to the strength of the medication, the wiser choice would have been only one pill.

Regardless of my medicated condition and per usual when we were alone on a trip, Edward's expectations were higher than normal. I somehow performed in my drug-induced state. As had been the case since my honeymoon night, I submitted to Edward and God.

Upon our return home I learned that our four children had all been very sick in our absence. When I saw their weary faces and heard Mac and Marion's account of everything that had happened, my heart ached with the thought that I had been away when they had needed me most.

The overall emotional and mental effect of our anniversary cruise on me was depression from feeling completely trapped and extreme desperation to escape my sexual obligation. My despair engulfed me in a fog black as night. I did not believe divorce was an option and I would never leave my children, so I began considering other means of escape from my relentless duty. To illustrate this reality, not long after we had returned home, I began seriously thinking about ways to decrease if not altogether eradicate Edward's insatiable drive.

As I grappled with my reality, I reflected on how I was not the only woman who had been so deeply and traumatically impacted by marrying a male in Edward's family. My sister-in-law, Elaine, who was also a submissive Christian wife and mother, had married Edward's older brother, Sam. She had suffered a nervous breakdown a few years after they were married and had several children.

Due to the fact that they had moved far north to a remote area of Canada shortly after we were married, I had only seen them a few times. Edward told me they had moved to get away from Mac and Marion's control. I had only heard stories of Elaine's emotional crisis from Edward and his parents. I remembered her as a very kind, soft-spoken woman.

During the dark night of my soul, I realized that Elaine had been up against the same emotional dynamics in her marriage. I put two and two together. Up until then I had believed Mac and Marion's incriminating story about her mental and emotional instability. During my desperate struggle after the cruise, I understood what had really happened to her.

I acknowledge that strategizing to reduce Edward's

drive was extreme behavior, yet I was extremely desperate to relieve myself of my dreaded duty. I began making calls to medical professionals to find out if castration could potentially lower or eliminate a man's drive. I was deeply disappointed when several professionals informed me that castration would not effectively change anything.

I did not keep my struggles a secret from Edward. I informed him I made the phone calls. Rather than seeing my desperation and cry for help, he looked at me in shock and anger.

"How could you do such a thing?"

"I couldn't think of any other way to change your sex drive. I'm always tired and I have no interest."

His angry face and cold tone of voice communicated everything as he stated, "I don't see what the big deal is. All you have to do is lay there."

In that moment I did what I had done countless times before. I surrendered to my reality and gave up any hope of freedom. I also resigned myself to the hard, cold fact that I would receive no mercy from my husband.

During the days, months and years that followed I lived in the dark night of my soul. For the most part I dissociated from my emotions to survive. I remember few details from those years. I know that from morning until night I performed my duties as wife and mother, constantly dreading having sex with Edward, to the point of feeling nausea at the mere thought. Trying to be the best mother to Lars, Sara, Violet and Jasmine and obeying God and Edward was all I knew.

Late in 1998 we began considering a move from the Northwest to Arizona. This idea resulted from Mac and Marion's concerns about their health, and they felt that living in a warmer, drier climate would be beneficial. Edward still worked for Mac and much of what we did and how we lived revolved around them, so we considered moving south with them.

After growing up in the cold Montana climate and living in the Northwest all of my life, the thought of warmer temperatures and sunshine appealed to me. I know my enthusiasm also stemmed from the feeling of being trapped day in and day out. I was desperate for any change that might bring light into my life. Living in a location where the kids and I could be outside in the sunshine sounded like blessed relief. Per usual, Mac and Marion were the ones who would ultimately decide our fate and we awaited their royal decree.

In March of 1999 Mac and Marion proclaimed that we would move to Arizona and their commercial real estate company would be headquartered there. We listed our home for sale and waited. I was eager to move and yet our large home out in the country was not an easy sell. I struggled to keep the house neat and clean in order to be ready for showings on short notice. Seven months went by with no offers.

In early October Edward decided he would change real estate agents if our home had not sold by the time our current agents' contract expired a few weeks later. I really liked our agents, a married couple named Robert and Jean, and did not agree with Edward's decision to terminate their contract. I felt they had worked hard to sell our home over the months and if anyone deserved the commission, they did. I prayed that a buyer would come along before their contract expired, enabling them to receive the commission.

As the deadline loomed, a showing was scheduled. We were told that the prospective buyers were a couple from Colorado. I had hopes that maybe they would appreciate our beautiful home, forest setting and country lifestyle.

On the day of the showing the kids and I went outside to play while the agents walked through our home with the buyers. We had gone through that routine numerous times over the previous months with no resulting offers.

On that particular day, the tour only lasted 15 minutes which I assumed was a bad sign. Typically, when prospective buyers finished the visit quickly, they were not interested. I stood outside by the swing set, holding two-year-old Jasmine on my left hip, as I watched the couple walk out of the house with their agent. The man, George, walked up to me and asked, "If I wrote you a check today, what would you accept?"

Those were the last words I expected to hear, and you could have pushed me over with a feather. I gave him a number, to which he agreed with a handshake, enabling Robert and Jean to receive the commission they deserved. The documents were signed the next day and we were given the move-out deadline of October 31.

Due to the fact that I had been gradually packing up our possessions for months, we were able to pull everything together in just a few weeks. Before we finally drove away on Halloween, I did a final walk through of our home. Leaving that beautiful place and all the precious memories with our children was very difficult, yet I had many painful memories I was eager to leave behind. We loaded up our van and U-Haul trailer, and headed south.

As I write this, a feeling of de ja vu floats across my mind as I flash back to my 6-year-old Self, walking down the plywood stairs of my new home in Montana. I felt happy and hopeful that my life would get better. I had similar emotions when we moved to Arizona. I was hoping against hope that somehow the change in location would bring about miraculous changes to my life. Although ultimately that would prove true, my hoped-for reality would take years to unfold.

PART TWO

You shall know the truth, and the truth
shall set you free.
– *Jesus*

SEARCHING FOR LIGHT

We arrived in Arizona in early November. Mac and Marion had built a luxury custom home on a golf course. Edward chose and purchased our home based on proximity to his parents. My home preference prior to moving to Arizona had been a for-sale-by-owner home a half hour away, which I had located on the internet several months before we moved. I had contacted the buyer who was willing to sell without any agent involvement. With 5 bedrooms the home was the perfect size and layout for our family, plus we would have saved significant money on the realtor commission.

Prior to making the final decision about our home purchase, Edward accompanied Mac and Marion to Arizona to meet with the seller. In spite of the fact that Edward acknowledged that the home was perfect for our family, Mac and Marion persuaded him that the distance of half an hour's drive was too far away from them.

Edward then found and purchased a four-bedroom

home five minutes away from their home. That scenario was just one of many times when my feelings and preferences were dismissed in favor of Mac and Marion. Twelve years into our marriage, his parents took precedence. The Arizona weather was moderate during the winter months and we all enjoyed the sunshine and swimming pool in the back yard. We visited several churches in search of a church family, including the large church attended by Mac and Marion. Edward and I both preferred a smaller, more intimate church and began attending a small Baptist church. I was homeschooling Lars, Sara and Violet at the time, and we joined a homeschool group for the purpose of socializing with other families and children.

We made some friends in our Baptist church and hosted a Bible study in our home. The temperatures rose about 90 to 100 degrees in May which made being outside for long periods of time impossible unless we were in the pool. The thought of being cooped up inside until November or December motivated me to look into areas where the temperatures were cooler. I learned of a recreation area in the nearby mountains where temperatures were cooler in the summer, so we decided to take a day trip.

After an hour and a half drive, we reached the mountain summit, and I felt the cool air wash over me like a balm. I breathed a huge sigh of relief. As I inhaled the delicious fragrance of the evergreen trees, a strong feeling of homesickness swept over me. I had lived in the Northwest my entire life and had no idea how deeply that area was engrained in me. The sights and smells of that mountain-top forest struck a deep chord within me, resonating like the feeling of home. To my surprise, six months after our arrival in Arizona, the sensation of homesickness began to seep into my consciousness.

After our trip to the mountains, we learned of a more expansive mountainous area four hours away called the White Mountains. In late May of 2000, we explored that region. The White Mountains were beautiful, and our family enjoyed every moment. Again, I felt so relieved to be out of the extreme heat, and comforted being surrounded by evergreens and mountains. Edward, being a woodsman from a young age, loved the area as well.

We took several trips there during the next few months and stayed in hotels. One weekend, Edward and I were sitting in the hotel hot tub. As I sat next to him, he wrapped his arms around me and held me in a tight grip, like a vice. "You're trapped", he stated. "You can't get away."

My immediate visceral reaction of fear was powerful and palpable. He attempted to brush off his comments as a joke. In spite of his attempt, I knew in the deepest part of my soul that his words were true. I had felt that chilling reality since our wedding day. Similar to that comment, another veiled phrase he used "jokingly" over the years to assert his authority was, "You have to love me. God says so."

After several months of staying in hotels during our trips to the White Mountains, I suggested we purchase a small mobile home for our weekend getaways. Although Edward was not enthused about spending the money, he ultimately agreed with the prospect of saving money on hotel costs over the long run. The three girls shared a small bedroom, Lars slept in the living room, and Edward and I slept in the other small bedroom.

Even though I still had to follow through with all my conjugal duties during those weekends, I looked forward to being in the mountains. Just the thought of being in the cool air amidst the evergreen trees helped me through the months of homesickness. Those breaks were an oasis in the midst of the desert, both physically and emotionally.

Edward informed me that Mac and Marion did not like the fact that we had purchased the small mobile home. My desire, which was not in accordance with their agenda, created a rift between us. When we moved to Arizona, their unstated expectation was that we would be available whenever they needed help, especially as they grew older. That had been their plan for Edward since he started working for Mac in his early twenties, and Edward was aware of that fact.

If we were four hours away, Edward could not readily be at their beck and call. For this reason, their feelings toward me, their "beloved" daughter, started to shift. The difference was clear whenever we saw them. I felt the emotional distance between us. I knew them well and sensed the intended chill without any words being spoken.

As I began pushing the boundaries of risking Mac and Marion's disapproval, the Universe gave me much-needed guidance one day in a used bookstore. A title in the psychology section caught my eye. The book was *Codependent*

No More, by Melody Beattie.[14] I read the cover and felt an intuitive nudge to purchase it. That book started a healing revolution in my life, ultimately resulting in profound and permanent changes. Edward did not like the fact that I was reading a "psychology" book. When he saw me reading *Codependent No More,* he would remark with a distinct air of disapproval, "You're reading psychology lies again?" He believed that modern psychology ran cross-grain to the principles of the Bible and were thus anti-Christian. I kept reading anyway.

With each page I discovered more about myself and the ways in which I needed to change in order to be emotionally healthy. I had never heard the term "codependent" before, and gradually I became painfully aware that I had been living that definition my entire life. If you are not schooled in the language of codependency, allow me to educate you.

Melody Beattie explained that codependency is a learned pattern of behavior motivated by impulses such as fear, guilt, pity and obligation which in turn drive actions which can be described as rescuing, fixing, pleasing and enabling. As I read *Codependent No More,* I discovered that codependent patterns of behavior usually develop during childhood through learned roles in the family. That had certainly been true for me.

Thanks to Melody and her life-saving book, I embarked on a long journey of learning how to be codependent no more. Over years my journey would guide me through

---

[14] Codependent No More, 1986

the very painful and ultimately freeing process of remembering and learning from my past. My life became like the famous quote by Lao Tzu, which says, "A journey of a thousand miles begins with one step." In 2000 I started taking my first, tremulous baby steps out of the thick, dark fog and began earnestly searching for light.

The second year in Arizona ushered in a new era for me, the beginnings of which resembled the dark ominous clouds, rumbling thunder and lightning commonly seen during the monsoon season in the desert. As is true of the monsoon, the rumbling and fury of my personal storm would transform my inner landscape, bringing new life. Melody Beattie's book was just the start of how the Universe would continually guide me into truth in order to set me free. In the midst of the darkness and continual emotional turmoil the Universe gave me clear signposts, directing me out of the thick dark fog and into the light.

The violent rumblings in my soul emanated from the extreme friction I felt with my husband and in-laws. I knew if I said anything to Edward about my strong feelings of homesickness or about wanting to leave Arizona, I would be met with the fury of the storm. The future proved I was not wrong. In April of 2001, I broached the subject of moving.

"What do you think of us moving back to the Northwest?"

Silence.

"Do you think it's a possibility?"

Silence.

Edward looked at me with a serious expression and spoke with a tone of finality, "No. There is no way we can move. We can't leave Mom and Dad. We moved here to be with them. Besides, the business couldn't survive if we moved."

His response was in keeping with every other response I had received during the course of our 14-year marriage when what I wanted was at odds with Mac and Marion's preferences. I seemed to have little to no chance of being heard.

During the following weeks we continued our bi-weekly trips to the mountains, and in spite of Edward's continual resistance, I persisted in bringing up the subject of moving back to the Northwest. Even though Edward was not enamored with the desert and extreme heat any more than I was, he dug in his heels whenever I asked him to consider the topic of moving. He had lived close to Mac and Marion his entire life with the exception of one year in college, and he did want to leave them. He also knew what would happen if we even suggested the idea to them.

Although nearly every other time in our relationship I had submitted to Edward or his parents, that time was different. I felt a continual urgency to press the issue. I sensed I was being guided by an energy beyond myself. At that time, I still called the energy God. Since then, I have changed my perspective, and now refer to the guiding energy as the Universe. Contrary to my Biblical programming, I now believe that the loving energy of the Universe is not subject to man-made rules and not connected to the threat of eternal punishment.

I brought up the idea of moving several more times and Edward finally conceded to broach the subject with Mac, although he was afraid to do so. He sensed the fury of the storm to come, as did I. Mac's reaction turned out to be exactly as we had anticipated. Edward returned from the meeting with a somber mood and ashen face. I stood in the kitchen of our Arizona home and listened as he recounted Mac's response to our suggestion.

"Dad and Mom believe you are emotionally and mentally unstable. They have discussed your behavior and think you may have something seriously wrong with you. They suggested you need to have a full panel of bloodwork done. They believe you may have a serious illness such as early Alzheimer's disease or a brain tumor. They also believe you might be having an affair or might be addicted to drugs or alcohol."

As I looked at my husband's serious face, not only was I in shock as I tried to absorb the words spoken by "Mom and Dad" I realized my husband believed what they said. After a few moments, anger started to set in. The people who for 13 years had proclaimed their love for me as a beloved daughter chose to gaslight me when I challenged their control. In spite of the fury within, I remained calm and simply looked at Edward.

He continued, "Dad suggested we talk to the counselor at their church."

"Excellent," I said. "Go ahead and make the appointment. I look forward to speaking with a counselor."

My cooperative response surprised Edward. He looked at me with a quizzical expression and followed through with scheduling the appointment.

I knew I was in no danger of having any serious illness so just to prove my point, I made an appointment with my doctor to have a full blood panel done. I went to my doctor's office and sat in the waiting room, calmly waiting to be called by the nurse. I will never forget that moment in time.

The wonderful nurse who drew my blood that day asked why I had requested a complete blood panel. I proceeded to tell her how my in-laws suggested I be tested based on the fact that I wanted to move back to the Northwest. She looked at me wide-eyed, shook her head and said, "Honey, they are waaayyyyy too far into your life." Hallelujah and Amen sister. Finally, a voice of reason and truth.

As I write this, I feel so much gratitude for the validation I received from that strong, kind woman on that day 20 years ago. Her voice was a clear signpost as I searched for the light. And, by the way, my bloodwork came back totally healthy. No indications of the disastrous possibilities that Mac and Marion had suggested, much to their disappointment.

One day I was given another clear signpost out of the blue. My dear soul sister from high school, Ella, managed to track down my phone number and called me. Although we had gone in different directions and had only seen each other a few times since high school, our soul sister connection and deep love for each other had never changed. The

Universe literally threw me a lifeline that day. Although I cannot recall the exact words exchanged between us, I remember the immense gratitude and relief I felt just from hearing her voice. I knew I could trust Ella and therefore dared to share my truth with her. As I sat on the stairs in my Arizona home, I spoke my story for the first time and confided in her about my struggle, pain and current situation. That was a big step in searching for the light.

I told her about the gaslighting, Mac and Marion's control, Edward's constant pressure for sex, and his punishing anger if I did not cooperate. When she heard about everything I was facing, she told me in no uncertain terms that I was living with emotional abuse. That was the first time I had heard those words used in connection with how I was treated. She was compassionate and empathetic, which was the opposite of what I faced with my husband and his parents every day. Her voice was another clear signpost as I searched for the light.

Before we met with our first counselor, Mac and Marion scheduled a meeting to speak with us in person. We met with them at their luxury home on the golf course. I explained to them why I wanted to move back to the Northwest. Marion looked at me and said, "After everything we've done for you?" She then added, "Who is going to take care of us?"

In June Edward and I met several times with a woman named Barbara, who was a counselor at the large church where Mac and Marion attended regularly. She was a kind woman and an excellent counselor. We spoke with her regarding the subject of our moving and about Mac and Marion's response to the idea.

Barbara also scheduled a session with Mac and Marion and soon discerned the truth. When she broached the subject of their behavior, Mac interrupted her. He informed her in no uncertain terms that they were not meeting with her to discuss *their* behavior. They were meeting with her only to discuss "what was wrong with Rae."

Based on that revelation, Barbara ended their session and declined to meet with them again. During my next individual session, she recounted her conversation with them.

"I confronted Mac and Marion about their behavior, and they were not willing to look at themselves. They told me they had only come to talk about you. I told them I would continue to meet with them only if they were willing to look at their unhealthy behavior. They chose to leave."

I will always be extremely grateful for Barbara's courage and ability to discern and speak the truth in our situation. She was the first counselor I consulted and the first person to defend me. She served as another clear signpost during my search for the light.

Along with my struggles regarding Mac and Marion and moving back to the Northwest, I also shared my very difficult sexual reality with Barbara. Other than Ella, she was the first person I had told during my 14 years of marriage. I told her about Edward's constant pressure and how I wanted a reprieve. I told her how he had purchased a motion detector alarm to set outside the kid's bedrooms so they could not come near our bedroom when we were having sex.

I shared with her how one particular day, Edward told me he wanted to have our scheduled time at his business office on a Saturday afternoon. At that time, I was suffering from significant back pain due to degenerative disc disease as well as bulging, torn discs in my low back. As had been true many times, he expected me to follow through in spite of my pain. In keeping with the past, I submitted and did my duty, knowing that any objection would be dismissed. As I lay with my back on the hard floor, feeling pain with each movement, I detached from my body and went away in my mind.

Another day, I was laying on the carpeted floor downstairs as Edward once again sought his fix. His efforts were especially prolonged that day due to the fact that he could not maintain an erection, causing him to become more frantic and angrier as time went on. He persisted in his attempts to achieve orgasm, while my back and hips throbbed with pain. For several days afterward, the pain in my lower back and hips made walking difficult.

Barbara recommended I draw a firm boundary with Edward by telling him I would not have sex with him for an undetermined period of time.

I told her, "I'm really afraid. He will be very angry. I've tried to tell him the same thing before and each time he became angry and silent".

She then told me something that I have remembered and endeavored to live by since that day. She said, "Try to never base a decision on fear." Little did she or I know at the time that most if not all of my life was, and always had been, based on fear.

Although I was terrified and already very stressed by the emotional pressure, I followed through and told Edward what Barbara had recommended. He responded with angry silence exactly as expected. His silent punishment was too difficult and painful for me, and I was not emotionally strong enough at the time to hold my boundary. I once again submitted to his desires.

In addition to my motives of avoiding Edward's anger and being a submissive Christian wife, another motive was the emotional and physical safety of my young children. As had been the case for years, during that time I was very concerned about how Edward's anger would affect them. If I did not cooperate with him sexually, he was much more likely to become angry and emotionally unsafe with them, and the opposite was also true. If I gave him his regular fix, he was calmer and happier. During that time, he was constantly on edge due to the tension with Mac and Marion and his volatility was clearly displayed several times.

One such incident occurred on a Sunday evening when we had returned home from church. Jasmine was around four-years old and a very active little one who pushed boundaries more than the other children. That night she behaved in a way that made Edward angry, at which time he picked her up and spanked her severely. For a few seconds I stood in shock as he unleashed his fury on her little body. After a few seconds I intervened.

"Stop!" I took Jasmine away from him.

In the space of 5 or 10 seconds, his severe actions had been enough to leave bruises on her.

Another evidence of Edward's emotional volatility occurred when loading our family van for a trip to the mountains. Our dog did something to incur Edward's wrath and he picked her up and threw her into the back of the van. The force of the impact caused her to cry out in pain and squirt yellow liquid from her bowels all over the inside of the van, which made Edward even more angry. Not only did I feel terribly about our dog's suffering Edward's violent behavior frightened me and our children. That event also triggered the memory from my childhood when I had witnessed Dad throw our hunting dog down the stairs. I felt the same terror as I had back then.

I felt so desperate regarding my obligation during that time in Arizona that I regressed to an emotional coping mechanism that I had frequently used during my youth to numb my feelings. I told Edward that drinking beer might be a way for me to relax and enjoy sex. Even though I knew my approach was risky based on his reaction to my drinking 14 years earlier, I felt desperate enough to risk his displeasure regardless of the consequences.

Much to my surprise I did not have to convince or persuade Edward. He bought beer for me and for a while I drank a few before having sex with him. To my disappointment, the effects of the alcohol were not enough to change my feelings of revulsion. Although I knew from many previous experiences during my youth that I could have consumed more alcohol in order to become completely numb, I did not want to do anything that would prevent me from safely caring for my children. At least I was sane enough to draw that line.

The next significant signpost that emerged in the thick, dark fog during my search for light came after Barbara confronted Mac and Marion about their behavior. Mac advised Edward to find a different counselor and to make sure that the counselor was a Christian man. Mac emphasized that Edward needed to call and interview several potential counselors to ascertain their beliefs and doctrines. Mac specifically instructed him to find a man that "Rae can't control."

Per usual, Edward unquestioningly heeded Mac's advice, ultimately choosing a male Christian counselor named Matt, in whom he felt confident. Before our first session, Edward promised me that he would heed Matt's counsel. If Matt advised us to stay in Arizona, we would stay. If he advised us to move back to the Northwest, we would move. I felt the weight of Edward's promise and the eventual impact Matt would have on our lives. I did not sleep at all the night before our first session.

We entered Matt's office for the first time in late June and sat on the couch across from him. Matt started the session by asking what he could do for us. In the next moment Edward wordlessly reached into his shirt pocket and pulled out a yellow piece of legal-length paper filled with notes.

"I've written down a list of Rae's behaviors that have been of concern over the past months. I'd like to share them with you," Edward stated as he unfolded the paper. Matt sat across from him, silently and calmly awaiting his disclosure.

Edward proceeded to read out loud the full page of notes he had written, which focused specifically on all of my "unstable, erratic" behavior. Basically, all the ways in which I was the problem.

In spite of my feelings of shock, I sat quietly and listened to Edward's total blindside. I kept my eyes fixed on Matt's face as Edward repeated all the lies that Mac and Marion had told him about me, speaking with conviction like he believed them. Although the deep betrayal felt like a knife going through my heart, I managed to remain quiet and calm. Matt sat casually in his chair, completely calm. During Edward's monologue, Matt shifted his gaze to my face now and then as he listened intently to Edward's words.

When Edward finished speaking, he looked at Matt expectantly. I am confident that he expected Matt to sympathize with his plight as the husband of a crazy woman. When Matt remained silent, Edward asked him, "Well, what do you think?"

Matt continued looking at Edward, remaining silent for a few more seconds. He then spoke these words directly to Edward, "I just want you to know, I'm taking notes on you, too."

I will never forget that powerful moment in time. I felt like the skies opened and grace poured down on me. My entire body relaxed with an enormous wave of relief. Matt had seen the truth about Edward. I knew I had an ally.

After leaving Matt's office, we stepped into the elevator. As the doors closed, providing privacy, I asked Edward why he had written the page of incriminating notes about me. He told me that Mac had advised him to write down all the details of my behaviors and to read them at the beginning of the session in order to prevent me from taking control. His revelation did not surprise me. Once again, Edward had obeyed Mac without a single thought for my feelings, only this time I had an advocate who saw the truth, and their scheme backfired. Another clear signpost had appeared in my search for the light.

Over the next few months, we participated in couples and individual counseling with Matt. As with Barbara, Matt was able to discern the toxic, controlling dynamic with Mac and Marion. In August, he gave us the recommendation that we separate from Mac and Marion and move back to the Northwest. Despite the fact that Edward was not happy with Matt's decision, he had no choice but to follow through after promising both me and Matt that he would heed his counsel. I felt vindicated and grateful beyond words. The Universe had come through with flying colors.

Edward told Mac and Marion the news a few days later. As expected, their reaction was anger and surprise. The first words Marion shrieked in her hysteria were, "What are people going to think?"

Although Mac pulled out some strong-arm tactics by threatening to shut down their real estate company and our family's sole source of income, Edward followed through with his promise. In spite of the fact that I communicated my willingness to see them and for them to spend time their grandchildren, I saw Mac and Marion only a few more times during the three months before we moved, and they chose to see the children only three more times.

One of the times I saw them occurred when they scheduled a meeting with us at their home right after Edward announced that we would be moving. They made one last effort at changing our decision. We sat at their large dining room table, with Mac at one end and Marion at the other, like king and queen of their royal dynasty. Marion pulled out the power of the Bible and referenced the part of the New Testament where Judas had betrayed Jesus to the Pharisees from Matthew, Chapter 26, by stating, "This just seems like Judas and Jesus."

I was clearly Judas, and they were clearly Jesus. In spite of her heavy-handed tactic, I remained unmoved. Their cruelty had changed me, and I was no longer the submissive woman who would bow to their bidding.

After their unsuccessful attempt to control out future, Mac and Marion quickly rallied for the purpose of image management. The next day they mailed a letter to their inner circle of family and close friends in order to put their spin on our news about moving. Their strategically worded letter informed everyone that Edward and Rae were moving because of Rae's "condition". They communicated that although they were "devastated", they had accepted our decision as "the will of God".

Everyone in their close circle of family offered them empathy. No one seemed to question their credibility. On the other hand, everyone questioned mine. At that point, I did not care what other people believed. I felt myself moving closer to the light and that was all that mattered.

RAYS OF LIGHT

The Universe faithfully and continually provided clear signposts to lead me through the storm. We moved out of our home in Arizona on Halloween, 2001, and drove away on November 1, exactly two years to the day when we had left the Northwest. When we arrived back in Washington the weather was cold and snowy, and I felt like I had died and gone to heaven. Edward, however, did not feel quite the same way.

For a period of time Mac continued his threats to shut down their real estate company as a result of our move. He assured Edward that the company could not possibly survive with us living in the Northwest. In spite of all his huffing and puffing, Mac did not blow the house down and contrary to his adamant prophecy that the business would collapse with Edward living at a distance, the exact opposite proved true. The business thrived more than ever before during the years that followed.

Edward had daily contact with Mac and frequent contact with Marion, which produced tension and strain between us. After everything they had done to gaslight, malign and discredit me, I had zero tolerance for them. Although I made myself clear by telling Edward I wanted nothing to do with his parents, I did not interfere in his contact with them, nor did I attempt to keep our kids from them. Our kids knew they were free to visit their grandparents if and when they wanted. Edward took Lars and Sara to visit them not long after we moved.

In keeping with our life history, we began attending church again soon after we moved. I became involved in a woman's Bible study and our kids participated in the children's program. We became members of the church and I was asked to be the speaker at the annual women's retreat. I was told the theme for the retreat was joy and I wrote my material accordingly.

Once again, my programming took over and the performer took center stage. Over the course of the four retreat sessions, I spoke of joy in my relationship with God and my joy as a wife and mother. I assured the women that as Christians our faith in God could enable us to tap into a deep well of joy in the midst of pain, grief and tragedy. In truth I was selling a bill of goods that I did not buy myself, which was what the performer did best. I regurgitated my programming and went through all the motions exactly as I had been taught. Smile, perform, and be the exemplary Christian woman.

As convincing as my performance was, the Universe would not let me get away with my façade much longer.

Healing and freedom cannot be known without truth. I would soon embark on the painful, life-giving journey of getting real about my marriage, myself and my life.

One significant way the Universe changed me was by introducing me to a woman named Christine at the women's retreat. She and I connected on a soul level the first time we spoke, and we began taking weekly walks together after the retreat.

By that time, I had discontinued homeschooling and our kids were attending public school, which allowed me more free time. Christine was a very kind woman and also direct in her communication. She openly asked me, "What is the secret in your marriage?" in reference to how I had spoken of joy in my marriage. She was struggling and wanted my advice.

Her question left me speechless. In that moment I knew I had a choice to either cover up with a façade and I had done my entire marriage or to tell her the truth. I sensed Christine was someone I could trust, and my truth just came tumbling out.

"I'm not as joyful as I appear," I told her. "I'm not happy in my marriage and I haven't been for a long time. I only spoke what the Bible says, and what I've been taught to say. That's what God wants me to do. Obedience is what matters."

I was completely real with Christine and she was completely real with me. I told her how I had dreaded sex with Edward my entire marriage and how he showed no concern for my feelings. She told me she felt the same way in her marriage. Looking back, I know that Christine's friendship and love were the Universe's way of preparing and supporting me to speak my truth in riskier ways in the future. She was a ray of light in my darkness.

The landscape of my life was soon to become dark and tempestuous again.

Thankfully, the Universe would not me settle for anything less than truth and freedom.

I became bolder and began speaking my truth little by little to Edward. He was still predictably defensive whenever I brought up the subject of sex and historically, I had always backed down when met with his anger. My energy started to shift, and I became bolder in speaking my truth in spite of my fear.

One morning as I sat on the edge of the bed, I stated how I felt.

"I don't feel like I have a choice about sex, and that feels abusive to me."

"How can you possibly use that word?" he asked in astonishment.

"That's just the way I feel. You don't care about whether or not I'm interested. You don't care about my feelings."

He ended our conversation by climbing out of bed, his angry silence once again dominating the atmosphere. I stayed on the edge of the bed, pondering our exchange and feeling grateful to have spoken my truth.

Another conversation took place when we arrived home from church one Sunday. On that particular day the pastor had spoken about the subject of sex in a way that emphasized a wife's role of submission to her husband. I did not agree with the way he had approached the subject, so I told Edward how I felt. He once again became defensive about my comments.

"What do you want from me?" he asked in exasperation.

I looked him in the eye. "I want you to back off on sex," I stated matter-of-factly.

He responded emphatically, "You are making a mountain out of a molehill. Do you have any idea how good you have it? Do you have any idea how many women would kill to be in your position? I earn a good income. I'm home every night and weekend. I'm faithful. I'm a good father."

Not only did he avoid my direct statement and deflect my request he dismissed me by highlighting his upstanding character traits and how good my life was because of him. He showed no willingness to give my simple request any consideration. I looked at him in silence, once again feeling the heartbreaking reality that my husband would not offer me a shred of kindness or compassion.

Another occasion when I boldly spoke my truth was with Mom which was uncharted territory for me. Unlike our normal conversations which usually remained superficial and directed by her, this conversation turned out to be extremely revealing in terms of my childhood programming. Although I typically remained silent about my personal life, I chose to broach the subject of sex and my struggles with Edward. I told her that I felt the way Edward constantly controlled and pressured me without sensitivity to my feelings was abusive.

Rather than offering empathy or understanding, she paused and redirected the conversation to her Christian motto, offering what she believed to be the answer to all of my problems.

As had been true all of my life with her, her tone took on the quality of a preacher in the pulpit. She advised, "Just think of doing it for Jesus."

Wow. I had heard a lot of preaching and Bible references from Mom over the course of 40 years, but the shock of those few words left me speechless. Had she really advised me to have sex with a man as a sacrifice for Jesus? A man who cared nothing about my feelings? Yes, she had done just that.

Tragically, her words represented the reality of what I believe still happens in many Christian churches and in many Christian marriages. In all of my decades of sitting in churches and listening to hundreds of sermons preached by men, I did not once hear a male pastor say that Jesus would never endorse any behavior that would coerce, guilt-trip, control, manipulate or use punishing tactics to force a woman to have sex.

Jesus himself defended and showed respect for women. He faced down men who used and abused women. I challenge anyone to show me anything different from the Bible. Along with being a woman's protector and defender, I believe with all my heart that Jesus would in no uncertain terms tell a woman to *never* cooperate with a man, sexually or otherwise, who does not treat her with kindness and respect. I believe he would tell a woman that her value lies in who she is, not in how she performs sexually or otherwise.

In spite of the verses in the Bible that may indicate otherwise, a woman always has the right and choice to say yes or no to man, regardless of who he is, including a Christian husband. According to the Bible Jesus sacrificed everything, including himself, to show his love. The very definition of a Christian man is the one who emulates Christ, which means sacrificing everything, including his sexual desires, to show his love.

Despite my shocked silence, Mom confidently believed her advice that Jesus would require a wife to sexually submit herself to man, even one who showed no consideration or respect for her or her feelings. Sadly, I believe she had lived that reality with Dad for her entire marriage. Even more to the point, she considered a wife's sexual submission to an abusive man as a spiritual sacrifice to Jesus. All I can say to that is, that is just tragic.

Although I received no assistance from Mom that day, the Universe had my back. I soon received miraculous assistance from another source, ultimately enabling me to break free from Edward's control and abuse, once and for all.

After 17 years of marriage, I continued struggling deeply in regard to my obligation with Edward, and I lived in constant dread. I could not stop the feeling of nausea that took over at the mere thought of him touching me. I dreaded hearing the sound of the garage door opening at night, announcing his return from work. As I had done since my honeymoon, I continued to cope through dissociation. I detached from my body and escaped to a different place in my mind. I would picture myself in a beautiful mountain pasture and recited the 23rd Psalm over and over in my head. Sometimes I cried quietly. All the while, my Christian husband only focused on his fix.

A discussion between us one day shone a spotlight on the fact that his only reason for marrying me was sex. The topic arose when I shared some news told to me by a friend about an elderly man in his 80's who was getting married.

Edward laughed and stated, "Why get married if you can't have sex?"

I stared at him incredulously.

He then casually remarked, "Well, why not just stay friends?"

There it was. The truth in boldfaced, unmasked brutality. Although I had intuitively sensed the painful truth about my husband since our honeymoon, after 17 years of marriage his statement somehow still shocked me. That was his only motivation for marrying me. Not our relationship. Not me as a person. *Sex.* Even when his blatant comments slapped me hard across the face, I did not have the ability to walk away. I still believed God required me to stay and be a submissive Christian wife until death do us part.

Once again, the Universe brought me a friend to offer me support and truth. In 2002, my friendship with Carolyn began through my role of volunteer in the library at my kids' school. Carolyn brought a ray of light into my darkness. Over time we became good friends and talked openly about our lives and marriages. I shared my struggles with her, and she also shared her struggles with me.

In the fall of 2004, after I had known Carolyn a few years, she told me she was pursuing a divorce. Since our lives and marriages shared similar dynamics, she gave me an article about emotional abuse that had been helpful for her. The title of the article was "The Silent Killer of Christian Marriages". The article was an excerpt from a book entitled *Healing the Hurting*.[15] I still have a copy of the article and will always be deeply grateful to the Universe and to Carolyn for shining another ray of light into my darkness.

I eagerly read the article when I was able to find some time alone. It accurately described the reality of emotional abuse in a Christian marriage. For the first time in 17 years my heart was opened to the depth of emotional abuse I had been subjected to my entire marriage. I was overwhelmed by the sense of relief I felt as I read the words. Rays of light poured into my prison cell.

The article outlined how Christian men use the Bible, anger and their position of authority as Christian husbands to emotionally and sexually control their wives. They are often supported by church leadership and as a result their wives have no one to turn to for help. The wives live in continual fear and entrapment with no way of escaping the abuse. The article went so far as to say that Christian wives who are emotionally abused view sex with their hus-

---

[15] Healing the Hurting, 1998

bands as degrading, and even a form of rape, because they and their feelings are dismissed and ignored.

Reading that article was the first time in my marriage that someone had actually put into words how I had felt every time I had sex with Edward since my honeymoon. The relief I felt was vast. The article also drew the conclusion that any woman who had been emotionally abused had essentially been abandoned by her husband and thus had grounds for divorce. The article recommended seeking out counseling before taking that step in the hopes of repairing the marriage. Divorce was only suggested as a final option.

After reading the life-changing article, I soon realized that I needed to act upon the new revelation of truth. Although my stomach was in knots and I could barely sleep as I contemplated Edward's reaction, I braced myself and shared the article with him a few days later on a Sunday morning. I felt sick as I watched the stoic, angry expression on his face.

His first words in response were, "Do you want a divorce?"

"No," I responded. "I want to go to counseling as the article recommends."

"I don't agree with the article." He looked me right in the eye and stated, "It's not me who has abused you, you have abused me."

I looked at him calmly and held his gaze. "Let's go to a counselor and let them decide that. I'm not going to have sex with you until after we see a counselor."

As had been true before whenever I drew a boundary, he responded with silent anger. That time, I held my ground and more rays of light poured into my dark prison cell.

In spite of the extreme tension between us that morning, we followed through with our Sunday routine. When we arrived at church, we smiled and greeted everyone as usual. We sat next to each other and gave the appearance of being a happy Christian couple.

As with our counseling in Arizona, Edward insisted on choosing our next counselor. Confident that the Universe would once again have my back, I did not resist his control. Shortly thereafter he was given a recommendation by a male Christian friend. His friend recommended a male Christian counselor named John. Edward scheduled our first session with John in the beginning of October 2004. As he had done with Matt in Arizona, Edward took control at the beginning and thoroughly explained his side of the story. John then asked me to share my thoughts.

I told him about Edward's relentless pressure for sex during out entire marriage and his lack of consideration for my feelings. I told him how Edward became defensive and angry whenever I asked for a break from sex. I told him how Edward had continually deferred to Mac and Marion during our marriage.

As I shared about the depth of my pain and struggle, I started crying. I looked out the window and away from Edward so he could not see my face. I rarely cried in front of him, knowing that he believed women cried for the purpose of manipulation. No doubt at that moment he believed that was my motive.

Thankfully John was able to discern the truth as Barbara and Matt had before him. At the end of that first session, he made a statement that brought more rays of light streaming into my dark prison. He recommended a 90-day abstinence period, emphasizing that a break was necessary considering the emotional duress I was experiencing. I felt such immense relief, like I had felt when Matt had been my advocate in Arizona.

Edward's expression of shock gave away his initial reaction. Clearly, he had not seen that one coming. I believe he was actually expecting John to take his side. He had never had anyone stand up to him and he was up against the proverbial wall. After all, John was the male Christian counselor he had chosen based on his good friend's recommendation.

Edward rallied in his own defense by attempting to build a case against me. He referenced my affair in 1989, 15 years prior and spoke the following words to John in the hopes of getting a reprieve from the standing judgment of abstinence. "She gave it to him, but she won't give it to me."

His argument had the opposite effect than he had hoped and did nothing but add to the list of reasons why the abstinence period was necessary. We left John's office experiencing polar opposite emotions. While Edward experienced anger, I felt overwhelming relief and gratitude.

The next few weeks played out with a great deal of tension between Edward and me. I started wearing pajamas to bed for the first time in my marriage. Although he was clearly not pleased, he did not resist. He knew John was my advocate. After our first session as a couple, I met with John for an individual session.

He counseled me to consider a separation from Edward if he was at all resistant to counseling. I was ready to do as he recommended if necessary. Edward chose to continue meeting with John and for a few weeks we seemed to be making some progress. That changed a few weeks later during one weekend while I was gone and Edward's sister, Tiffany, stayed with him and the kids in my absence.

I had gone away for the weekend with a good friend from my church named Jill who brought more rays of light to my dark prison. We had traveled to Portland to attend a Christian women's conference. Jill was a certified marriage and family therapist who compassionately validated my feelings and was very supportive and encouraging regarding the path I was pursuing with counseling. I felt more hopeful and positive when I returned, but those feelings soon faded when I was met with the opposite energy as I re-entered my home to find Edward sitting in the living room, writing in his journal when I walked in the door. He barely acknowledged me and continued his writing with zeal. His anger was palpable.

Over the weekend he had shared with Tiffany about our counseling and everything John had recommended. As his older sister and the one with whom he had always shared the closest relationship among his siblings, Tiffany had a strong influence over him. He usually followed her advice with equal obeisance as with Mac and Marion. She and her husband were conservative Christians just like the rest of the family. While I was away, she convinced Edward that John's counsel went against Biblical teaching. When I returned home, he was very sullen and withdrawn.

The next morning, while we were eating breakfast together, I asked him why he was angry. Edward stared out the window.

"Something dark and evil is happening with John," he stated.

"What do you mean?" I inquired.

He proceeded to tell me all about his conversations with Tiffany over the weekend. His anger felt unsafe to me and I began wondering if I had serious cause for concern. For the first and only time, I looked in his journal to see what he had written the previous night when I had returned home. I needed to know if the kids and I were safe.

What I saw was impossible to unsee. He had written, over and over in bold, underlined capital letters, "I HATE HER, I HATE HER, I HATE HER, I HATE HER..." Although I was very concerned to see the blatant words on the page in his handwriting, I admit I was not surprised due to the fact that his energy had been clearly telling me the same thing for quite a while, especially since I had drawn the boundary with sex. I felt the best thing to do was to remain calmly vigilant and take one day at a time. Thankfully, he chose to continue counseling with John and eventually his energy shifted back to a less angry, more cooperative attitude.

Prior to seeing John, I had pondered the possibility of

Edward being a sex addict. His behavior was certainly the behavior of an addict. If he did not get his fix, he became increasingly angry and volatile. When he did get his fix, he became happier and calmer. His erratic behavior played out one night after we had gone to bed. He could not sleep and eventually got up and stood by the side of the bed. I knew he was standing there and yet pretended to be asleep.

"Can we have sex?" he asked.

"No," I replied.

He then left our bedroom and did not return that night. I was determined to not follow him. I was done trying to please or rescue him. Although I still had the memories of his behavior at the Baptist camp in my mind and was scared of what he might do, I was well acquainted with his emotional tactics and refused to submit to him, come what may.

The next morning, Edward told me he had gone down to the barn to sleep on the stack of hay. He also told me he had taken his gun down with him and had considered taking his life. Whether or not that was actually true, I do not know. At the time I sensed that he was only trying to manipulate me back into my place of submission.

I was not swayed by his tactics. Yes, I was still afraid of him, yet I was getting stronger in terms of standing my ground and not letting him intimidate and manipulate me. I did not know how I would do it, but I was determined to dig myself out of the dark prison in which I had been living for more than 17 years, even if I had to do so one spoonful of dirt at a time.

SPOONFULS OF DIRT

During my journey I read a book that described healing from complex trauma like digging out of a prison cell one spoonful of dirt at a time. That visual resonated in terms of how I felt as I struggled to become free after decades of fear-based programming and oppression. I had spent so many years imprisoned in pain, fear and grief.

Because trauma occurs when the victim has no voice and no choice, healing requires the exact opposite emotional dynamic. I had to start taking my power back and creating a life where I exercised my voice and my choice. Although becoming free seemed like an unachievable goal, I had enough light to see my reality more clearly, giving me hope and courage.

Edward and I continued with couple and individual counseling through 2004 and into 2005. As in the days after I had given birth to our babies, I was well aware that Edward was eagerly counting down the days of abstinence which constantly perpetuated my familiar feelings of anxiety and dread. Once again, we were on opposite ends of the emotional spectrum.

During one of my individual sessions with John, I told him that I did not want to feel pressured by Edward to perform at the end of the abstinence period. The 90 days came and went, and I did not feel anywhere near ready to resume my former obligation. In fact, I still felt physically ill with just the thought of Edward touching me, which I eventually learned was a clear physiological symptom of trauma.

As weeks went by, however, my Christian programming began chipping away at my resolve with the familiar influences of guilt and obligation. I was not being a good Christian wife. I was not obeying the Bible. I once again succumbed to the belief that I needed to obey God regardless of how I felt and decided to try to push through my feelings of aversion. I thought to myself, *maybe I will feel different. Maybe the abstinence period helped.* Regressing into my old pattern, I forced myself to perform and once again found myself living in constant dread. My aversion had not diminished even a little.

After pushing myself to perform for several weeks, I told Edward that I could not have sex with him anymore. I told him that my feelings had not changed in spite of the period of abstinence and as long as I felt that way, I would not act in a way that went against my feelings. That declaration was my first big spoonful of dirt.

Shortly thereafter, he approached me while I was sitting in the living room reading a book. He sat down next to me on the couch with his open Bible.

With a caring tone of voice he said, "I'm concerned about your relationship with God. If you don't obey, your relationship with him will suffer."

He then referenced the all-too-familiar Bible verses from Ephesians Chapter 5 and 1 Corinthians Chapter 7 regarding a wife submitting to her husband and how the wife's body belongs to her husband.

I looked at him calmly and considered my response. I stated with conviction, "I'm not going to have sex with you no matter what God or the Bible say. If my relationship with God suffers or he chooses to send me to hell, then so be it. I'll have a conversation with him someday if or when I get the chance."

That moment was another huge spoonful of dirt. Although I still felt fear as I spoke those words, I also felt an infusion of strength and freedom. Edward clearly felt the opposite. He looked at me in disbelief. I believe in that moment he was struck with the realization that after 17 years of controlling me with the Bible and fear, his dictatorship was over.

We continued seeing John for counseling through 2005 and I was deeply grateful to have him as my advocate. Edward knew he could not get away with his old tactics of manipulation and intimidation, and his behavior began slowly changing. Although his continual focus on money and work remained the same, his anger became less overt.

After reading the vitriolic statements in his journal,

hearing his statement of marrying only for sex, and after years of being subjected to his manipulation tactics with the Bible, I did not trust Edward. However, I was grateful for a more peaceful home environment for myself and the children and I had no intention of divorce. At different times our girls had asked if we would ever get a divorce and we had confidently told them no. I no longer felt obligated to honor my marriage vow out of duty to God, yet I had every intention of keeping my promise to my children.

In December of 2005 John told us that he was going to discontinue counseling for a while and referred us to another counselor named Samantha who specialized in trauma counseling. We began couple and individual sessions with her in January of 2006. Although I did not fully understand the depth of my trauma at that time, I knew that type of counseling was exactly what I needed.

As my years of counseling with Samantha unfolded, I learned that as a result of the long-term emotional abuse and sexual abuse I had experienced during both my childhood and adult years, I had developed symptoms of complex trauma or complex PTSD (C-PTSD). Through my own research I learned that C-PTSD is different from PTSD in that C-PTSD develops as a result of long-term exposure to trauma, whereas PTSD typically results from a single, short-term trauma such as a natural disaster or accident.

Complex trauma is common in survivors of abuse who are subjected to emotional, physical and/or sexual abuse with no hope of escape. Often the abuse takes place in the context of interpersonal relationships where there is a real or perceived power imbalance, which certainly had been true for me. Not only had I felt trapped with emotional abuse in my childhood home I had felt trapped in my marriage.

After I learned the truth about my trauma and all the emotional damage I had accrued in my marriage, I felt more determined than ever to dig out of my dark prison. My hidden self, alone in the thick, dark fog, had been telling me the truth for years, yet I had always overridden her strong messages based on my programming and fear of God's punishment.

By the beginning of 2006, I had made progress in digging myself out of my prison cell, yet my excavation had just begun. Our counseling with Samantha continued and was the first time that Edward had not controlled the selection of our counselor. Although he was not pleased with seeing a woman counselor, he did not resist John's recommendation. During one of my initial sessions with Samantha, she made her assessment of Edward clear.

She did not mince words. "Edward is an angry man. Are you sure you feel safe with him?"

I carefully considered her question. "I know he is an angry man. I have felt that reality our entire marriage. At this point I do not believe he will hurt either me or the kids."

Samantha responded with both grace and concern. "I will respect your feelings and I also want you to assure me that you will leave him if you feel that you and the children are in danger."

I assured Samantha that I would heed her advice, and she did not try to control me or make my decision for me. She knew that my ability and choice to have control over my life was critical for my healing process. Dictatorial control with no consideration for my feelings had created my trauma and my future path required the exact opposite.

During one of my individual sessions with Samantha, I shared an article I had read about Narcissistic Personality Disorder (NPD). I remember her looking at me silently, her empathic expression conveying her understanding and the fact that the information was no surprise to her.

"The issue with NPD is that people with personality disorders rarely change, especially those with NPD," she said. "They view themselves as right and on a plane higher than everyone else, like God." In my experience that had certainly been true with Edward, Mac and Marion.

She looked at me seriously and said, "Are you sure you want to do this?" referring to my choice to stay in my marriage.

As I looked at Samantha, I carefully considered my future. "I believe that staying with Edward is best for the kids," I explained. "A two-parent home provides the most stability for them."

As had always been true, Samantha did not resist or try to control my decision. Her consistent support over the next five years provided me with strength and courage as I dug out of my prison, one spoonful of dirt at a time.

Now that I was armed with new knowledge and could see more clearly what I was dealing with, I gained more confidence in standing up to Edward. I finally understood that I was not the problem or the inferior one, nor had I ever been, and that clarity gave me determination. From that time on a fierce energy rose up inside me, giving me the courage to stand my ground and fight for my goals, which were my healing and my children's well-being. My fear did not go away. I simply chose to make choices based on courage instead of fear.

Back in the day when Edward had total control over me, all he needed to do was show a slight hint of anger or panic to nudge be back into submission. That was then, and that was history. With my newfound confidence, I began taking more time for myself. I spent one night a month at a hotel and with the kids being older, they were not as concerned when I left them, and I was not as concerned about them. Between the time I was away from Edward and the money I spent on myself, my behavior was a big change from my pattern of submission. I delighted in each moment I had to myself and every time away represented a spoonful of dirt.

Another means through which I continued to dig out of my prison was by pushing boundaries regarding spending money in other ways. As with our entire history together, Edward was consistently controlling with money. He always had one predictable response whenever the kids or I wanted to talk to him about spending any amount money. We would approach him and the first words out of his mouth were, "How much does it cost?" We always had to negotiate and plead our case before he would concede to spending a single penny.

I clearly remember one day when he and I were taking our daily walk together I brought up the subject of spending money on something for the kids. His response was, "I feel resentful of how you and the kids spend my money." In one short sentence he revealed his true feelings. The kids and I were drains on "his" money.

Although I had known that sad truth for a long time, in that moment I felt grieved by Edward's obsession with money. I decided to press the money issue further.

I asked him, "How much money would you need to have in the bank before you would stop worrying?"

He replied, "There's probably no amount that would prevent me from worrying. The more I have, the more I will worry."

Edward's stress about money was something to which the kids and I were constantly subjected. Regardless of how much money we had, he never reassured us regarding our financial stability. In contrast, he frequently emphasized his stress levels and lamented that "we'll end up living under a bridge someday, eating potatoes."

His reference to homelessness was a veiled attempt to scare the kids and me into embracing his Scrooge mindset. In spite of years of his continual predictions of doom and gloom, quite the opposite proved true. We always had enough resources for a comfortable roof over our heads and the ability to purchase more than just potatoes.

I continued to push the boundaries regarding spending. Each encroachment I made on his Scrooge territory gave me another spoonful of dirt. At that time, we had money in savings, and my spending was not endangering our financial stability. So, I challenged the status quo one day in 2008. I was running errands in our older-model Subaru station wagon, when I drove past a used car lot and spied a sleek, dark gray Dodge Charger displayed in the front. My heart skipped a beat and I felt drawn to that machine like a magnet to steel.

I went home and told Edward I wanted to test drive the Charger. In spite of his immediate reaction of resistance, I was not deterred. I persisted in my negotiations and we drove to the car lot. I took the V-8 Charger for a test drive. As I sat in the driver's seat and experienced the power of that machine, I felt pure joy. Although Edward was less than thrilled with the idea, he reluctantly agreed to trade in our practical car. Every time I drove my Charger, I felt a surge of freedom. That car was another spoonful of dirt.

Another way I negotiated with Edward for money was in regard to family vacations, which I scheduled and planned every year. If the choice had been up to Edward, vacations would not have happened. As a result of my proactivity, we typically traveled to the Oregon coast in spring or summer.

In 2008, I thought a family trip to Hawaii would be extra special. The kids were ages 17, 16, 14 and 11 at the time, and I thought they would enjoy the adventure. I pushed the financial boundary and Edward finally agreed.

The oceanfront rental home was fantastic and the

scenery breathtaking. I remember sitting on the veranda gazing at the exotic landscape, watching the waves crash against the rocky coast. Although I had never witnessed such lush beauty before, I struggled to emotionally connect to the natural beauty around me. Nature had always been my refuge yet being on vacation with Edward increased my emotional stress. He never took his mind off money and work, even on vacations, and I always felt his underlying sexual angst more during trips, keeping my nervous system on high alert. In spite of my emotional reality, the kids enjoyed the vacation. Being able to make that trip happen and giving them that joy was another spoonful of dirt.

The next challenge in my excavation process may sound trivial and insignificant to most people, yet for me altering the daily chore of making breakfast for Edward presented another means through which I carved out a spoonful of dirt. Since we had married, I dutifully prepared his breakfast on weekdays which involved cooking hot cereal and serving toast with orange marmalade along with a small glass of juice. The routine never altered. The realization that Edward, being an efficient and productive adult, could easily make his own breakfast dawned on me like the morning sun, giving me clarity and the determination to rid myself of that obligation.

Prior to broaching the subject, I sensed I would be met with resistance. My intuition was spot on.

I told Edward, "I don't want to make your breakfast anymore. I feel that is something you can do for yourself."

His facial expression immediately communicated

shock and displeasure. As I had witnessed countless times before, his body stiffened, his face grew serious, and his eyes dark. Without a word, he made his feelings about my declaration crystal clear. He knew I was serious and did not argue with me. I did not change my stance and from that day forward I was only responsible for my and the kid's breakfast.

In 2009 I took another significant stand by informing Edward that I would not be attending church anymore. I would no longer go along with anything that felt like performance to me. I would not perform any longer to earn love from anyone, even God.

In place of my life-long habit of church attendance on Sunday mornings, I indulged in hanging out at a bookstore or in a movie theatre. I relished my new Sunday morning routine. The movie theatre was usually empty and the tickets less expensive than during peak hours. The feeling of sitting in a dark theatre on a Sunday morning watching the movie of my choice, especially the R-rated ones, felt luxurious. I munched on popcorn, savored my freedom, and celebrated another spoonful of dirt.

Along with insisting on my freedom from the life-long tradition of church attendance, I insisted that our kids were old enough to make up their own minds about church as well. Although Edward chafed against my insistence, our kids were all for the idea. After I took a stand on their behalf, they stopped going to church unless they wanted to go with Edward, who continued attending every week. What mattered to me was that they felt free to choose and were no longer subjected to the performance-based belief that they were only acceptable and loved if they sat in a church building. That large spoonful of dirt increased freedom for them as well.

When Mom came for a visit, she asked about our church attendance, and I told her our kids and I were no longer attending church.

She looked at me with incredulity and asked, "How will they learn about the Christian faith and God?" she asked, eyebrows arched in shock.

"They are old enough to decide on their own and can attend church with Edward whenever they want," I explained. Even though I could tell she clearly disagreed and wanted to contradict my decision, she was aware I would not tolerate any control regarding my choices, and she chose to respect my boundary.

Her awareness of my intolerance for disrespect and control stemmed from a situation that had occurred with my three siblings. For healing purposes, I had chosen to write an email to Ted and Seth to confront them about their disrespectful, abusive treatment of me during childhood which had continued into my adult years. By then they had both become successful businessmen who absolved themselves of any responsibility and replied in a return email that their behavior had been "typical.".

Not only did they clearly communicate disrespect and dismissal with their words they chose to attach a cover letter addressed to Edward and sent both emails to his email address rather than responding directly to me. First and foremost, they wanted to convey their desire to continue their relationship with Edward. Through their alliance with him, they showed themselves to be the same men who had shown no respect for me and my feelings my entire life. I chose to detach from them, and I have never regretted that decision.

In spite of the fact that I had intentionally asked Ted and Seth to keep the matter between us, they chose to tell Viv. As I suspected would happen, Viv attempted to play intermediary and tried to resolve the matter by quoting Bible verses to me. She admonished me to forgive and forget. After having known her as a controlling big sister my entire life, her tactics were no surprise.

However, she underestimated who I had become after facing down long-used Bible-based control and manipulation from Edward and his parents. I was angered by her attempt to control me and I clearly communicated that my decision regarding Ted and Seth did not involve her. I gave her the ultimatum of acknowledging that her behavior was unacceptable and of refraining from any further controlling behavior, or she would receive the same response as Ted and Seth if she chose to dismiss my request.

Unfortunately, Viv believed she was right, and she did not change her approach. I in turn followed through with discontinuing any communication with her. Although my decision to disconnect from her caused me pain, I would never again tolerate her or anyone else's control in my life, especially through the means of Bible-based manipulation.

My decision to detach from Viv was validated a few

years later when I learned through the grapevine that she had stalked me on the internet. Although she was no fan of modern self- help books, she knew Melody Beattie was one of my favorite authors and she somehow discovered my name amidst the many readers who commented on Melody's daily blog.

Unfortunately, I was not tech savvy enough at that time to know I should use a false name. I had been commenting on the blog for more than a year, sharing private information about my life with other people who had experienced similar pain and trauma. Between my real name and the other personal details, Viv managed to put together the pieces. She then chose to share my private information with Seth, who then contacted Edward, who then told me. Even I was shocked at the level to which she had stooped to gain information about me.

A few years after I learned of her internet activity, Viv contacted me through email, wanting to "start over" in our relationship. I informed her that I knew of her subversive internet stalking and betrayal, and due to the fact that I could not trust her, a reconciliation between us would not happen.

She did not acknowledge or take responsibility for her actions or apologize for violating my privacy and sharing my private information with men I did not trust. Taking a stand and confronting my siblings was an extra-large spoonful of dirt.

The last significant spoonful of dirt that I will share involves the subject of my hair. You may remember how

I wrote earlier about the fact that I was Edward's ideal woman in terms of physical characteristics, which included my long hair. During the years of our marriage, he had insisted that I keep my hair long. If I even hinted at cutting my hair or doing something different, he reacted with predictable anger.

After John and Samantha became my advocates, I found the courage to stand up to him and do what I wanted with my hair. Over the years I tried a variety of shorter hairstyles. Although hair changes may seem trivial and inconsequential to some people, for me they symbolized freedom from dictatorship. Edward had controlled me for so long in regard to my hair that every time I did what I wanted, I carved out another spoonful of dirt from my prison.

In essence, every choice I made to stand up for myself and every time I used my voice and my choice to say what I wanted was another spoonful of dirt. Every choice represented progress in my goal of digging out of my dark prison. My freedom was worth every spoonful I intentionally carved out between 2004 and 2010. Little did I know in the spring of 2010 that I was on the verge of breaking out of my prison. There was one more obstacle standing between myself and liberation, and I would need help breaking through that final blockage. As always, the Universe sent me assistance at just the right time.

LIBERATION BEGINS

My liberation began with the first of two unexpected conversations which produced what I would best describe as emotional detonations within me. Those explosions transformed my inner landscape and ultimately broke apart the large obstacle that stood between myself and freedom.

The first inner explosion detonated during a vacation to the Oregon coast with my daughters, Violet and Jasmine. They were 15 and 13 at the time. We had traveled as just the three of us for several reasons. First, due to many stressful and unpleasant vacations with Edward, I decided I did not want to take any more trips with him. Second, Sara and Lars were otherwise occupied and unable to join us.

The three of us enjoyed our time together in a lovely rental home near the beach. We spent our days by the ocean, sightseeing, shopping and eating out in restaurants. I believe that was the first time I genuinely relaxed and enjoyed a vacation.

One evening I sat across from Violet and Jasmine in a restaurant booth. We were casually talking about anything and everything when one of them dropped the emotional bomb by saying, "Mom, we think you need to get a divorce. We know you've been unhappy for a long time and we just want you to be happy."

I stared at them, stunned and speechless.

I scrambled to get my emotional feet under me. I collected my thoughts enough to say, "Do you have any idea what that would mean? A divorce would be very hard on you, and I can't put you through that. I promised you I would never do that, and Dad won't want it."

The response I received from my heroic and loving teenage daughters was, "Mom, we'll be fine. We just want you to be happy. If you're happy, we're happy."

My life would never be the same.

My daughters' words terrified me. I could not begin to fathom how I could possibly go through a divorce, let alone have my children be subjected to the process. The girls and I did not discuss the subject any further for the rest of the trip.

Although the thought of freedom from Edward enticed me like a tantalizing fantasy, I was in too much shock to seriously consider the concept let alone verbalize my thoughts to anyone else. I could not run my children through a divorce, no matter how much I wanted freedom. My role was to protect them. As much as I loved Violet and Jasmine for wanting my happiness, I could not heed their advice. I did not tell them about my silent resolution.

I did, however, start taking more time away for myself that summer. I needed some distance from Edward. In July of 2010 I decided to travel three hours to my old college town for the weekend. That weekend was so helpful in terms of reconnecting to the young woman I had been 23 years earlier. She was still a real, albeit dormant, part of me. I could feel her happiness and freedom when I walked and hiked through my old stomping grounds.

Sadly, I reflected on the reality that I had become someone very different in the years since then, and not in positive ways. Just being in my college town woke up the part of me that had been buried alive in 1987 when I married Edward. I remembered how our counselor, John, had once told me, "Who you've become is not necessarily who you are." He was right. As a result of my codependent, fear-based behaviors, I had become someone very different than who I am.

During that soul-searching weekend I spent some time in the college library and happened upon a book entitled *Something More: Excavating Your Authentic Self.*[16] As I read the content which described the process of discovering my authentic self, I knew that was the reason why I had traveled back to my college town. I had some serious excavating to do. That book fanned the almost extinguished embers of the independent young woman inside of me and created a slow burn that eventually became a flame, fueling my passion for freedom.

---

[16] Something More: Excavating Your Authentic Self, 2000

When I returned home after that weekend, I felt less tolerant of the constrained ways in which I had been living for so long. Like the title of the book, I knew and felt there was something more. Since 2004 and for the greater part of six years, I had not felt any change in my sexual feelings toward Edward. My body still responded involuntarily with nausea at just the thought of his touch.

I had slept in the same bed with Edward for 23 years and dreaded getting into bed every night, even without the possibility of sex. I wore thick men's pajamas to hide the form of my body in order to prevent his arousal. I slept with vigilance on the outer edge of the bed. I would involuntarily startle if he came too close to me. I had done my best to continue sleeping in the same bed for the simple reason that I knew our kids would worry if I slept somewhere else.

One night an event occurred that showed me that in spite of my kid's concerns, I needed to place a high priority on sleeping in a separate place. While I was asleep Edward rolled toward me and put his arm across my chest. I awoke with an intense rush of adrenaline and jumped out of bed before I had even registered what had happened. I stood by the side of the bed, my heart racing. The next day I told him I needed to sleep in a different space, which was a challenging situation considering all of the bedrooms were occupied by our kids at the time.

I started to think creatively and came up with the idea of purchasing a small trailer or camper which could be placed behind our home. That would be my private space. Edward was not enthused about my idea for two reasons. I would be moving away from him and I would be spending money. In spite of his displeasure, I purchased a used camper. To solve the dilemma of no plumbing, I set up a luxurious porta potty. I ran a long extension cord for electricity. Violet and Jasmine assisted me with transforming the drab interior into a colorful, inspiring butterfly theme. I thought of that small space as my transformation chrysalis.

I know some people may think of life in a camper as a demotion in status. However, I can honestly say with every fiber of my being that when I started sleeping and spending time alone in that little camper I was in absolute heaven. The solitude was delicious and as far as I was concerned there was no better place on earth. I had not had a private space away from Edward to call my own for 23 years. As an introvert, I desperately need alone time to recharge, and I had not been given or experienced that necessary health component for most of my marriage.

I could breathe and relax within that blessed space. My nervous system finally had the opportunity to rest without the threat of involuntarily being thrown into panic mode. I still feel overwhelming gratitude for how that little camper provided me with increased freedom, healing and peace.

By August of 2010 I assumed Violet and Jasmine had forgotten all about our earthshaking divorce conversation. I soon found out that I had assumed incorrectly and had also underestimated the determination of my teenage daughters. One day while we were sitting at an outdoor café in a beautiful park, enjoying the summer weather and scenery, they spontaneously revisited the subject. As with the first conversation two months earlier in Oregon, the second one blindsided me from out of the blue. They repeated the same words they had adamantly delivered to me in June. "Mom, we think you need to get a divorce. We know you've been unhappy for a long time and we want you to be happy. If you're happy, we're happy." Like Winston Churchill and his motto of "never, never, never, never, never give up," Violet and Jasmine proved to be relentless in their crusade for me to be free. I have told them many times since then that they are my heroes. Their loving support and encouragement were the critical pieces I needed to give me the strength to break through the final barrier into freedom.

As I continued to reflect on the future and Violet and Jasmine's persistent message, I had the sobering realization that if I chose to stay with Edward, they would watch me intentionally choosing to stay in an unhappy marriage. Like my Mom before me, I would be repeating an unhealthy generational pattern. More importantly, I knew that if I set that example for my daughters, they would be more likely to follow in my footsteps. That thought was very sobering and provided me with the much-needed courage to rise up and fight my battle for freedom. I would do everything within my power to fight not only for my freedom, but for my daughter's as well.

During my next session with Samantha, we discussed the subject of asking Edward for a divorce. I sobbed during most of that session. The emotional weight of all the years during which I had struggled and fought to survive came to the surface. I had also doggedly clung to the hope that Edward would become the prince I dreamed he would be. Kind, compassionate, genuinely concerned for my well-being. In essence, I came face-to-face with the realization that I had to let go of my Snow White happily-ever-after ending, once and for all.

After almost 24 years, I had finally come to the end of my clinging to my childhood fantasy and chose to face the brutal reality that I had been blocking out since our honeymoon. There was a part of me that desperately wanted to be free and there was another big part feeling deep grief as I contemplated the end of my marriage. My family would never be the same again.

Samantha looked at me with so much compassion. She knew what Violet and Jasmine knew. I needed to get a divorce. I told her that I could not fathom how I would broach the painful subject with Edward. Not only had we been married for more than 23 years we shared a substantial amount of emotional and physical investment in common. Four children, a home and property, as well as financial assets including two real estate properties. I literally felt like conceding defeat before I even started.

In order to give me strength to follow through with the initial battle charge, Samantha suggested writing a letter to Edward. In contrast to the thought of trying to communicate my thoughts verbally, her idea felt manageable, and I followed her advice.

I wrote and hand delivered the letter to Edward in

September of 2010. We were sitting outside on our deck as we had done many times before. I was terrified, and my heart was breaking. I felt like I was having an out-of-body experience. I cried while Edward read the letter.

He read the entire page in silence, with his familiar stoic expression, showing no emotion.

His first words were, "Are you going to take the kids from me?"

I responded quietly, "No."

His next words were, "Will you make me move out of the house?"

Again, I responded, "No."

That was that.

From that moment on Edward took charge of the divorce process. He wanted to keep our divorce private from everyone, including family and friends. He wanted to keep living as if nothing had changed. I did not oppose his request. He also wanted to wait two years before we told our kids, claiming that his reason was to shield them from pain. At that point he did not know about Violet and Jasmine's persistent conversations with me and their encouragement regarding the divorce. He assumed they knew nothing, and I did not contradict him.

Although Violet and Jasmine were the catalysts for the divorce, they feigned ignorance. Sara eventually picked up on the truth and also kept the knowledge to herself. The only one who was surprised by the news was Lars. He had never been one to notice or get involved in the emotional nuances or drama in our home. In fact, he made a point to proactively steer clear of drama, which I understood and respected. Growing up with three younger sisters, I certainly could not blame him.

By far the hardest part of the divorce was watching the pain my kids suffered as a result. Although I truly believed that my choice would ultimately be the best for everyone, we went through several years of turbulent waters before the storm started to die down.

Edward became more dependent on the girls for emotional support as I detached from being his main support, which was hard and stressful for them. I had felt the weight of being his emotional caretaker for more than two decades and I struggled with the awareness that he was now laying that burden on them.

Of the four children, Sara struggled most deeply with the fracturing of our family and Edward leaned heavily on her as his friend and confidant. Of all our kids, she was the most deeply entrenched in the same Biblical beliefs as Edward. At one point she asked me not to pursue the divorce. My heart broke as I saw the deep pain on her face.

"Mom, please don't pursue the divorce. Please."

With every ounce of compassion in my heart I told her, "The very last thing I want to do is hurt you. My heart breaks as I see your pain. But I truly believe taking this step will be the best for all of us. I wouldn't be doing this unless I believed that with all my heart."

Sara just looked at me wordlessly, pain and tears covering her beautiful face. In the weeks that followed a distance grew between us, the likes of which I had never felt.

She believed the divorce was solely because of me.

Not long after that conversation with Sara, I stood in the kitchen and asked Edward to tell Sara what really happened in our marriage.

"I'm losing my daughter," I said. "I want you to tell her the truth."

Edward did speak to her and although I have no idea what he said, the situation between Sara and I improved a little after that. However, a few more years would pass before she and I were able to have a close relationship again.

Approximately three years after the divorce, Sara told me she finally understood the truth about Edward and why I had to pursue the divorce. Her newfound awareness resulted from spending time with him alone during an extended overseas trip. I honestly did not care how she had received her epiphany. All I cared about was the fact that I had a relationship with her again.

I went along with everything Edward required for the divorce in order to keep the peace and shield our kids from pain and conflict as much as possible. In keeping with his desire that our divorce be a private as possible, he hired his business attorneys to handle all the details. Edward had done business with them for several decades and trusted them to maintain confidentiality.

In October of 2010, we met with his two attorneys. In regard to our money, Edward insisted that everything stay the same and we maintain joint bank accounts. The lawyers did not recommend this detail, yet Edward stood firm. The lawyers explained that per the law, all assets had to be split 50/50 in five years at the latest. Although I would have much preferred to have our finances split at that time, I chose to go along with Edward's stipulation. I knew any conflict regarding money would cause a great deal of turmoil and most likely delay the divorce process. Child custody was agreed upon 50/50. Edward insisted our divorce papers be filed in an adjacent county so the divorce announcement would not appear in our local newspaper. Both of the veteran attorneys who handled our divorce said they had never witnessed such an uncomplicated, uncontested divorce agreement in all their years of practice, which was saying something considering one of the attorneys would soon retire after 30 years of practice. The papers were filed and the mandatory 90-day waiting period in the state of Washington commenced.

That was a long and tense time of waiting, during which Edward and I continued to take our daily walks together. Again, that practice would not have been my first choice, yet I did everything within my power to keep our relationship peaceful and our regular walks were a part of my intentional agenda. One day, he stated, "I keep hoping that something would happen, like an accident that would put you in a coma, so that when you woke up you wouldn't remember the divorce."

Although on the inside I felt slightly alarmed, I stayed calm and kept walking. I had not forgotten the incident with Edward and the children at the Baptist camp forty years prior. I had a fleeting thought of what he might do to stop the divorce, which I quickly dismissed. By then I was well accustomed to pushing unsettling thoughts out of my mind.

In spite of a few minor delays, the divorce became final in March of 2011, thankfully without any life-threatening accidents to impede the process. Edward and I went for our regular walk on the actual day the papers finalized, and his mood was somber.

I chose to focus on the reason I had gone through with the divorce.

"I'm doing this because I believe the divorce will ultimately be best for all of us."

Edward remained silent for a few moments, and then said, "I don't agree that this is best for all of us."

Once again, we were on opposite wave lengths. Ultimately, four years later, after he was happily remarried, I received communication from him stating that he agreed that what I had said was true. The divorce had been best for everyone.

Although the divorce was final and my liberation had begun, I would eventually realize that the divorce was only the beginning of my long walk to freedom.

THE LONG WALK
TO FREEDOM

My long walk to freedom started uneventfully by continuing on with daily life the same as prior to the divorce, the only difference being that I was no longer married to Edward. Once again, this fact was due to my intentional agenda to keep the peace. Although I would have much preferred to move to another location and get distance from Edward, the girls preferred I stay and continue living in the camper. I agreed to do so only to provide emotional stability for them. I bought groceries, cared for the dogs, cooked meals, and performed domestic duties as before. I still co-owned the home and carried on with mutual chores as I had done before the divorce.

I continued traveling to my college town every other weekend to have time away from Edward. He consistently told the kids that he believed we would get back together one day. He continued wearing his wedding ring to make an outward statement of his commitment to me. I knew that a reunion would never happen, yet for the sake of our kids I tried to remain friends with him. In September of 2011 Lars moved away from home to attend college and the girls continued living in the house with Edward.

In January of 2012 I met a man named Gene at a coffee shop during one of my weekend breaks in my college town. He seemed nice and lived on a large ranch. I began exercising my freedom by dating someone for the first time since my divorce. A long-distance relationship worked well for me since I was used to traveling every other weekend anyway.

Two weeks after I met Gene, he asked me to put some of the utility accounts for his ranch, such as internet and electricity, in my name. He assured me he would reimburse me for the costs. The reason he gave for his special request was that he needed to "get off the grid" in order to elude some unethical business partners who were trying to track him down and sue him. He promised me he had done nothing wrong, and I gave him the benefit of the doubt.

In April of 2012, a little more than a year after the divorce, I decided to change my living situation. My sole reason for staying on the same property with Edward had been the fact that the girls preferred me being there. By 2012 they were 20, 18 and 16 and they understood that I needed to get my own place. I moved to an apartment five minutes away and continued to see them on a daily basis.

During the spring and summer of 2012, I continued traveling to Montana to spend time with Gene. Violet and Jasmine were supportive of my relationship with him and eventually traveled with me to the ranch. They loved spending time at the scenic homestead and traveled with me several more times for weekend visits. In July of 2012 Gene gave me what appeared to be a large solitaire diamond ring to symbolize our commitment. Not long after I began wearing his ring, Gene's energy started to shift. From the beginning of our relationship, I had described to him the behaviors of the men in my past that had caused me deep pain and damage. At the top of my list of unacceptable behaviors were anger and control. I told him I would in no way tolerate either as they were the most powerful emotional triggers for me.

Six months into our relationship Gene not only stopped paying part of what he owed me for his home expenses, he also started pressuring me for money. In August of 2012 we took a two-week road trip in his large motor home, during which a costly repair was necessary.

Gene informed me, "The repair is going to cost $2,000. I think it's only fair that you pay half since we are on vacation together and you're enjoying the motor home as well."

"But it's your motor home," I responded. "I don't think I should have to pay for something that isn't mine."

"You don't have to pay for hotel costs during the trip which would cost a lot more. You're actually saving money."

Unfortunately, I went ahead and paid half of the repair cost.

Not long after the vacation, Gene asked me to invest in solar panels for the ranch, to the tune of $30,000. One day as he enthusiastically described the improvements he wanted to make as soon as he had the funds, he turned the conversation into a request.

"I'd love to put solar panels on top of the barn. Just think how we could live completely off the grid without relying on the power company for electricity. Since this will be your home one day, what do you say to investing the money for our future?" he proposed with a big smile.

"But my name isn't even on the title. What would happen if I didn't move in or if something happened to you?" I questioned. "I would have no assurance of getting my money back."

"Why wouldn't you move in?" You said you want this to be your future home."

"I'll consider investing the money if you agree to putting my name on the title of the ranch."

Gene's mood shifted in an instant, his enthusiasm turning to brooding silence. I felt his angry energy when I resisted his control. As had been true my whole life, my involuntary nervous system shifted into high alert. I became more vigilant for any signs of anger from him.

During our first six months together, Gene remained respectful of my feelings and boundaries. However, after he had given me the ring and we had passed the six-month point in our relationship, he began displaying more overt anger and control while being increasingly dismissive of my feelings. As the weeks passed, I felt and noticed more behavioral and emotional shifts and continued to communicate my feelings and boundaries.

When he chose to show up significantly late for dinner

one night after promising he would meet me at a specific time, I challenged his dismissive, disrespectful behavior. He looked at me and said, "Why are you making a mountain out of a molehill?" I had heard those dismissive words from Edward back in 2004. At that point, I sensed the end was near.

In February of 2013 I informed Gene that I would be moving out of my apartment and purchasing a small home near where my girls lived with their dad. He became angry. "I thought you would invest that money in the ranch since this will be your future home," he stated.

"I'm buying the home to be close to my girls and as an investment for the next few years," I responded. "I will do what I want with my money."

He responded with angry silence and that was the final nail in the coffin. After more than a year with Gene, I exercised my freedom by walking away.

Although the break-up was painful, there was absolutely no way I would tolerate the same behaviors that I had been subjected to for most of my life. The girl and woman who had lived in the thick, dark fog had worked too hard to break free. She would not go backwards.

Although my relationship with Gene did not turn out the way I had hoped, I gained several long-term benefits from my year-long experience. Shortly after the break-up, I did a reality check with myself and carefully considered how I had contributed to my pain. I knew I had to refrain from blaming Gene and instead take full ownership of my choices in order to change and experience something different in the future. As difficult as the revelation was, I realized that my subconscious programming and codependent behaviors were still driving the show to a great extent. From day one I had jumped into a relationship with Gene without a thought of getting to know him first or protecting myself. I naïvely believed every word he told me from the beginning. I put his ring on my finger believing he was my prince, and we would live happily ever after.

As I considered my lack of awareness and codependent choices, I determined that if I ever chose to enter into a relationship again, I would give myself time to observe a man's character instead of readily believing his words. Rather than throwing a pity party, I threw a get smart party. I was not interested in another relationship. I had zero interest in locking myself in another prison. In fact, I did not know if I would ever trust a man again.

The Universe brought me an incredible book after the break-up to show me the truths that I needed to learn from my experience with Gene. The book is entitled *Women Who Run with the Wolves* by Clarissa Pinkola Estes.[17] If you are a woman and you have not read this empowering book, I highly recommend you do so. If you are a man who wants to better understand women and how to support female empowerment, I recommend you read it as well. There is no other book that has been such a powerful force in my life for bringing truth, awareness, healing, empowerment and guidance for cultivating a deep, authentic life.

The author studied and used the lives of female wolves

---

[17] Women Who Run with the Wolves, 1996

to illustrate how we are to live intuitively in strength and wisdom, connected to our authentic selves. She refers to the instinctive spirit of a female wolf as Wild Woman, who we as women are meant to embody as well. The author states, "The comprehension of this Wild Woman nature is not a religion but a practice. It is psychology in its truest sense: *psukh□/psych*, soul; *ology* or *logos*, a knowing of the soul."[18]

The book explains that, like female wolves, we need to listen to our intuition to carefully look for and discern truths beyond surface appearance, which is exactly what I wish I would have done from the beginning with Gene. The author also draws on myths and legends to teach deep truths to guide us on our intuitive journey.

I still frequently read this book to remind me of the path I need to walk in order to stay connected to my soul as the main source of guidance and healing. Although I no longer fully embrace the Bible-based teachings of my youth, *Women Who Run with the Wolves* has shown me the importance of remaining teachable and open to guidance from others, which brings up my next point. If I had listened to Lars' concerns regarding Gene, I may not have incurred as much pain. His was one of the voices trying to come through to me with the truth.

Although I had been fooled by Gene's façade, Lars had not. He first met Gene after we had dated for about six months. Although Lars has always been a pretty easy-going guy who gets along with just about anyone, he felt a

---

[18] Women Who Run with the Wolves, 1996

strong aversion toward Gene from the get-go. Upon meeting him about six months into our relationship, Lars sensed Gene's true character and the reality that he was only after my money. In the end, Lars' intuition proved accurate. My programming and naïveté had prevented me from seeing the dark, subversive truth. In hindsight, I was able to see the obvious red flags that should have alerted me to Gene's true motives from the beginning.

In spite of my painful learning experiences, I ultimately received increased freedom as a direct result of Gene's subversive intent. During the course of my relationship with Gene, Edward heard through the grapevine that Gene was only after my money and became alarmed about "his" money. Since we still held joint bank accounts per Edward's requirement, he knew that his share of the assets could potentially be at risk through me.

In order to ensure that Gene could not get his hands on any of his share of the assets, Edward proactively drew up a legal agreement in September of 2012 for the complete separation of our assets. Once again, I did not resist or argue with him in any way. His plan made possible a great deal of progress on my long walk to freedom.

Another conclusion I came to after my first foray into dating was that I did not want to commit to a serious relationship. I was tired of working so hard, only to end up with pain and loss. I planned to mail the ring back to Gene when Violet and Jasmine suggested I have an appraisal done at a jeweler to find out the value. I did so and found out that the "diamond" was a fake and the setting worth only a few hundred dollars. Fool me once, shame on you. Fool me twice, shame on me. I was determined never to play the fool again.

After a few months of nursing my wounds, I made some choices that helped me gain momentum on my long walk to freedom. In May of 2013, I invested in the small house that was close to where my girls lived with Edward. I enrolled in an 11-month program for massage therapy. I also decided to start dating "just for fun", which in the long run taught me to be careful how I defined fun.

The whole next year consisted of perusing online dating websites and choosing to date guys who seemed to promise fun. I would go out with them, have a few drinks, sometimes have casual sex, and then move on to the next guy. The difference between those guys and Edward was that I was now choosing where, when and with whom. The liberation was thrilling.

What I failed to comprehend during my joy ride was the reality that there were serious dangers lurking in the dating scene and I was still rather naïve and vulnerable. A yet deeper truth that I did not comprehend was that I was intentionally seeking out the thrill of danger for the specific purpose of distracting myself from my emotional pain and trauma. As long as I was distracted by the thrill or self-medicated, I did not have to think about or feel anything from my past. Turns out my behavior was predictable. Survivors of trauma often intentionally engage in risk taking behaviors with the specific goal of running from or distracting themselves from their pain.

Unfortunately, my running only served to accumulate more pain which caught up to me with a vengeance. I dated numerous guys from March 2013 to May 2014, had unprotected sex quite a few times, typically while inebriated, and did not give one thought to the potential dangers. Needless to say, that was not smart.

In May of 2014, my carefree attitude hit a brick wall when I felt some serious pain "down un-dah". I casually passed off the discomfort as a UTI resulting from all my nefarious activities. I made an appointment with a doctor, expecting to receive the routine prescription for antibiotics, enabling me to go merrily on my way. After the exam, she told me that she was not sure about my diagnosis and ordered a blood test.

A few days later I received a phone call with a diagnosis that I did not suspect.

"Hello? Is this Ms. Miller?"

"Yes."

"This is Sally from Doctor so and so's office. I'm calling to let you know we got back you blood test results, and you tested positive for herpes."

Silence. I paused in an attempt to absorb her blunt statement.

"Ok. What does that mean? What should I do now?" I had zero clue about herpes let alone what to do about such a diagnosis.

"We recommend you start taking an immune supplement such as L-Lysine and make an appointment with the doctor to discuss long-term medication to help control outbreaks."

I was still scrambling to make sense of her words. "Ok. I'll do that. Is there a cure?"

"No, I'm sorry. I'm afraid there is no known cure at this time."

"Ok. Thank you."

I hung up the phone and stood motionless, staring out the window. There was the ugly truth. My free-for-all lifestyle had landed me with an incurable STD and vagina on fire at the age of 48. In one brief phone call my year of carefree living officially came to a screeching halt. My chain had been yanked in the biggest way and I needed to get a serious grip on reality.

Living and learning can be a real bitch sometimes. I spent the next two weeks not sitting down because of my cranky nether region. Those weeks gave me a lot of time for reflection. Note to self: *Make smarter choices while exercising your freedom.*

In spite of the fact that I was confident one of the men with whom I had cavorted during my carefree year most likely knowingly passed along the special gift, I took the high road by contacting as many of them as I could in order to give them the happy news that they might want to get tested for herpes. I chose to offer that courtesy in the event that they had not been the culprit who gave me the gift. I also hoped my choice would potentially protect any other unsuspecting or naïve victims. Needless to say, my once-busy phone fell silent in the wake of my revelation.

I chose to tell my daughters about my crash collision with herpes. They were 22, 19 and 17 at the time. We had talked openly about relationships and I knew at least two of them were most likely sexually active. I wanted them to know that safe sex is not just a nice suggestion, it is a way to avoid a very painful and life-altering reality. As a middle-aged woman with hopefully four to five decades left to live, my reality with herpes seemed insignificant in comparison to the thought of them living with such consequences for the rest of their lives. I did not want them to experience the same pain or have their futures affected in the same way.

After so many years of remaining silent, alone in my desperation, pain and suffering, I adopted a new life motto. Always keep it real. *Always.* Own and embrace every part of myself, even my cranky va-j-j. *No more parts left alone and hiding in the dark.* I would hold my head high, herpes and all, as I continued on my long walk to freedom.

I also chose to tell my soul sister, Ella, about my flaming encounter with herpes. After not having contact for a few years, she got in touch with me right after my breakup with Gene in February 2013. She lovingly accepted me through all my crazy choices during my carefree year. As had always been true, she kept right on offering me compassion and support, never judging me throughout those messy months.

After my painful herpes wake-up call I re-entered the world of being a responsible adult and decided to sign up for counseling once again. I found a wonderful therapist named Jillian whose office was located near where I lived. Like Samantha, she also specialized in trauma recovery.

During my first visit, I recounted the journey of my life, highlighting the past year leading up to my diagnosis of herpes. She confirmed that my risk-taking behavior had been an emotional mechanism for avoiding my pain and trauma. She looked at me compassionately and said, "What do you want?" I stared at her with a blank look on my face.

After her million-dollar question, Jillian remained silent and patiently waited for me to discover my answer. In my mind I picked through my life's wreckage and slowly uncovered my five-year old self in the living room, acting out her Snow White fantasy. That little girl looked at me with a knowing grin and a warm feeling washed over my heart. *She knew.*

"What I want...what I have always wanted...is a loving relationship with a kind man who genuinely cares about me," I told Jillian about my long-buried dream.

She smiled and replied astutely, "Well, sounds like you've been settling for less than what you want." That was the understatement of the century.

With my excavated childhood dream in hand and a new resolution in my heart, I picked myself up and continued on my long walk to freedom. My next step was to start researching my options in terms of dating with my recently acquired physical companion. To my surprise, I discovered there was a popular dating website created specifically for people with herpes. Violet lovingly dubbed my new exclusive club, "Team Herps". Now that I was a full-fledged, card-carrying member of the team, I began showing up for practice. I pulled myself up by my bootstraps and created a dating profile.

SNOW WHITE RETURNS

After graduating from massage school in June 2014, I began working at a spa as a massage therapist. I loved the job as well as the soothing environment and friendly people. I was determined to earn a living and make a new life for myself. To begin with, I knew I had to live in reality and not wait helplessly for my prince to save me.

Ok Snow White, new game plan. No falling asleep and being helpless. Eyes and ears wide open. I knew I needed to create my future, not wait for a man to create my life for me. I needed to know and express what I wanted, and I needed to learn from history.

I let my five-year old self tell me what she wanted in her prince. She created a list with the qualities of respectful, kind, compassionate, able to connect emotionally, mature and honest. He would be a man I could trust.

Along with carefully describing what I wanted, I endeavored to be honest about myself. I wanted to confidently show up as my authentic self and not pretend or perform any longer to please a man. The first quality I highlighted about myself was that I am the proud mother of four amazing adult kids, and they are the top priority in my life. I knew that my prince would appreciate my commitment as a mom, and he would love my kids. Those were non-negotiables.

I highlighted a few key qualities about myself such as I am independent, honest, and I also emphasized that I am averse to clutter and do not want to be responsible for cooking, cleaning and doing laundry for anyone but myself. I wanted an equal partnership with a man who took responsibility for himself and his life, as I did for mine.

In July 2014 I chose to celebrate my freedom and my 49th birthday with skydiving. Melody Beattie wrote in one of her books that skydiving had enabled her to feel the sensation of letting go in a way like no other. That sounded like just what the doctor ordered, so I asked my daughter, Sara, to accompany me on a skydiving adventure since she had already had the experience of skydiving solo. Although I would have loved to have had the confidence to jump solo as she had done, I did not feel as brave as my 22-year-old daughter, so I arranged for us to jump tandem with instructors.

When we arrived for our jump, were given a few hours of instruction and then we squeezed into the small airplane with the pilot and our instructors. When we reached the altitude for jumping, my instructor connected my harness to his, which was equipped with the parachute. He then opened the side door on the plane and instructed me to place my right foot on the outside running board with him following suit. Feeling the force of the wind and looking down at the earth thousands of feet below was such a glorious rush. We rocked back and forth three times and on the count of three he pushed me out of the plane. I truly do not have words for the beauty of those moments. As soon as we left the plane, I let go of fear and focused intently on the joy of the moment. My takeaway from that exhilarating experience was that I want to embrace the same attitude I adopted when I jumped out of that airplane. I want to carry that sense of letting go and freedom with me even when my feet are on the ground. The quiet voice inside said *Let go of fear. Just trust.* For me that choice represents true freedom.

I met a prince candidate on the herpes website in September of 2014. His name was Allen. He looked friendly and healthy in his photos, so I contacted him. He responded positively and after a few weeks we met for dinner. When I saw him, my first impression was that his profile photos did not match reality. Allen quickly assured me that he had the goal of losing 50 pounds and getting in shape in the near future. Unfortunately, I once again believed a man's words instead of waiting to see if his actions followed suit.

A few weeks later Allen invited me out to his small, rustic home in the country where he lived by himself. When I drove down the driveway, I was immediately head-over-heels in love with the forest setting and the quaint little log home. I stepped out of my car to find a beautiful, linen-covered table on the front porch with wine, flowers and candles and a stunning view of the surrounding forest. As if that weren't already impressive enough, Allen proved to be an excellent chef.

When I commented that I did not enjoy cooking, Allen looked deep into my eyes while holding my hands in his and smiled saying, "You will never have to cook again."

That was a hard offer to pass up. We sat on the porch as the full moon rose, sipping wine and reveling in the beauty of the evening. In spite of only having known him for a month, the magic of the night overrode my better sensibilities, and I chose to believe his princely promises.

As had been the case with Gene, I communicated with Allen about my history of trauma with men. I made myself clear in terms of the behaviors that were strong triggers for me. I told him that I would not tolerate anger or control and I asked him to be sensitive to those areas. As with Gene, he seemed attentive for a while and for the first nine months our relationship felt overall positive.

In June 2015 I moved in with Allen at his rustic country home. Jasmine had just graduated from high school and was planning to move out of the area soon. Since none of our kids were living with Edward anymore, I felt free to sell my house and move a half hour away. I loved Allen's place in the country, and he needed help paying the rent. The timing worked out well for both of us. The natural setting was idyllic, and I sincerely had high hopes for our future together.

In January of 2015 I had been forced to resign from

my position as massage therapist as a result of neck pain and necessary surgery. I could no longer work as a massage therapist due to the fact that my neck problems were aggravated by the physical work required. Fortunately, a friend connected me to the job of veterinarian assistant which sounded like a lot of fun. The job required only a 10-minute commute from home, and I would actually be paid for hanging out with animals. Win/win.

Soon after I had moved in, I sensed an energy shift with Allen. He struggled with significant financial issues that he did not tell me about until I moved in with him. One day while I was sitting on the front porch, enjoying the tranquility, he approached me and asked for a loan of $500, assuring me he would pay back the money as soon as he sold his ATV and trailer. Against my better judgment, I loaned him the money, regretting my decision a moment later. He paid me back within a month and I told him I would not loan him money again. I sensed his displeasure when I drew that boundary and a rift slowly started to grow between us.

In the summer of 2015, I celebrated my 50th birthday by fulfilling a long-held dream of mine. I completed a motorcycle endorsement course and bought a motorcycle. Four years prior I had walked through a Harley Davidson store in my college town during one of my weekend getaways and had seen a beautiful black leather jacket. I bought the jacket that day and set my intention to wear it for the first time while riding a Harley motorcycle on my 50th birthday. That jacket hung in my closet for four years until I completed the two-day endorsement course. I proudly wore my jacket and rode my Harley Sportster on my 50th birthday. Snow White loved trading her traditional feminine garb for black leather. What a fantastic feeling of freedom. It was the next best thing to free falling.

I owned that motorcycle for four years until 2019 at which time I decided I did not want to take any more unnecessary risks with my body and my health. My two beautiful grandchildren had been born in 2017 and 2019, and I wanted to be able to enjoy them and my precious kids and friends for many years to come. Although I chose to part ways with my Harley, the times I spent riding that motorcycle gave me amazing memories of freedom that I will never forget.

During the latter part of 2015, I became increasingly disappointed in Allen's lack of follow through in relation to promises he had made early in our relationship, including cooking and weight loss. His excuses for not following through on his promises were typically that he was tired or did not feel well.

Another issue of concern that emerged was Allen's anger. Although he did not direct his anger at me, he frequently expressed anger with a loud voice about problems at work or politics. I do not deny that anger is a valuable emotion when necessary, in terms of being emotionally healthy. The issue I have with the expression of anger is when someone indiscriminately unleashes their anger in uncontrolled ways at innocent bystanders or without consideration for others.

I had felt afraid of male anger in my home for most of my life and I would not allow another man to poison my home environment with anger again. I asked Allen to stop blasting his angry energy while he was around me, even if his anger was not about me. Sometimes he listened, and sometimes he did not. His lack of respect and consideration for my feelings became an increasing concern.

In May 2016 I stepped up and spoke honestly with him about my struggles in our relationship. I described my disappointment and how I felt like I did not matter to him when he failed to keep his promises. I told him I needed a partner who was on the same page and who knew the importance of backing up his words with actions.

He sat at the top of the stairs while I stood below, looking up at him. He stated matter-of-factly, "I don't think I'm the man that you need."

As I looked at him and although his words caused pain, I had to agree. With a heavy heart, I ended our relationship and found myself at yet another painful crossroads.

In June 2016 Allen moved out of state for employment and I took over the lease on the little rustic country home. Between my job and money in savings, I could afford the payment and enjoyed living there by myself. After the break-up with Allen, I felt tempted to remain alone in my forest hideaway forever. In spite of that fantasy, I decided I wanted to keep my commitment and returned to Team Herps.

In early July of 2016 I received the gift of attending a truly magical wedding. My wonderful son, Lars, married his beautiful wife, Zoe. Set on Zoe's grandparent's farm against a backdrop of magnificent, giant evergreen trees, their wedding was like something out of a fairy tale. Lars and Zoe exchanged their vows with a depth of love and authenticity I had never before witnessed in a ceremony. Sara, Violet and Jasmine were members of the wedding party and my heart overflowed with deep gratitude as I watched Lars and Zoe exchange their vows. I was beyond thrilled to have Zoe as a part of our family.

I stayed open to future possibilities and met another man named Brian in September of 2016. He seemed friendly and upbeat. He invited me to his grandson's birthday party the following weekend and I agreed to attend. There, I met his daughter, grandson and granddaughter. His grandkids were very cute, and we had fun. He appeared to be a man who truly loved his family which was especially attractive to me.

After that evening Brian was very communicative and eager to spend time with me. As with the other men I had dated, I communicated to him about my relationship history and how anger and control were two behaviors I would not tolerate. Also, in keeping with the men before him, he seemed attentive to my boundary for the first six months, and then his energy shifted when I would not cooperate with his agenda.

I felt the shift in April 2017 when I made the decision to buy a house that needed remodeling. Brian had remodeled several homes and offered to help me with the renovations. I was grateful for his offer since I had never handled a remodel by myself. Brian and I had also talked about him moving in with me that summer when his apartment lease ended.

To proceed with the remodel. I made appointments with contractors and other workers and Brian accompanied me to those appointments. I received bids from several contractors for the construction aspects and also a bid from a painter for painting the interior. After reviewing several options, Brian and I agreed on the contractor that we felt was most knowledgeable and would do the best work.

The painter was a different story. I felt confident about the painter and told Brian I was going to hire him for the job. Brian thought the painter's bid was too high and said we should do the painting ourselves to save money. I had done a fair bit of painting houses in the past and I was determined not to do any of the painting that time around. I stated confidently that I would be hiring the painter.

Brian instantly went from being solicitous and loving to silent and withdrawn. I sensed the significant change in his energy immediately and my involuntary alarm system kicked in full force.

We were on a phone call when I told him that I would be hiring the painter to do the interior painting.

"I've decided to hire the painter. I think he will do a good job and for me it's worth the extra money. I don't want to do any of the painting myself."

Brian was silent for several seconds and then responded, "You don't care at all about what I think."

That's not true," I told him. "I appreciate your input.

However, I have the right to do whatever I want with my house and my money, and I'm going to hire the painter."

Again, silence. "Well, if that's the case, then you won't be needing my opinions anymore." He hung up the phone. That conversation took place in the morning and I did not hear from Brian for the rest of that day, which was a glaring deviation from his normal behavior. Thankfully, I had learned my lesson well by that time and was strong enough to stand my ground on the knowledge that I could choose to do whatever I wanted with my money. I was not going to stay in another relationship with an angry man who punished me with silence when I did not cooperate with his agenda.

I ended the relationship with Brian the next day and his last words to me were, "You're going to lead a sad, lonely, miserable life. Goodbye."

Although I did not agree with his prediction of my future, I appreciated his communication as an overt validation of his true character. I felt proud of myself for walking away.

I was re-writing my Snow White fantasy. Instead of waiting for a prince to awaken me, I was committed to waking myself up, little by little, through learning from all of my choices. Every day I made the commitment to staying awake as I moved toward a new life.

SNOW WHITE REWRITTEN

I moved into my "new" home in June 2017 and entered into a master's program at the nearby university in September. I had wanted to pursue a graduate degree for years and my time had finally come. My goal was to finish in two years and enter the job market. Those plans changed when during my first semester I decided to change programs from Applied Behavioral Analysis to School Counseling, for which I felt better suited. The switch pushed my graduation date out two years to May of 2021. Although that sounded like a long time to be in school, I figured four years of learning would be an excellent growth opportunity, especially in my 50's, which has certainly proven true.

The School Counseling program focused on a combination of psychology and helping young people, two areas about which I am passionate. During the course of my schooling, I was given excellent opportunities for learning and personal healing. As I learned how to counsel and offer healing to young people, I received healing as well. I am deeply grateful to know that when we experience our own healing, we are much better able to help others.

After getting settled into my home and schooling, I took a step back and evaluated the three relationships that had ended in the six years since my divorce. All along the way I had been walking toward freedom and yet there was something that did not resonate as freedom as I considered my choices. I took to heart the truth that I was the common denominator in all of my failed relationships. That proved to be an excellent, albeit difficult, exercise in understanding myself and my trauma.

As I reflected, I gave myself credit for all I had learned and how much I have grown with each relationship. Each one had given me valuable opportunities to learn and implement my learning. However, I had a sense that there was something driving my choices that eluded me, and I wanted to become aware of that unknown piece. I somehow sensed I was still asleep in some mysterious way.

I had read books about people who had histories of trauma and kept returning to the same type of unhealthy kind of person in an endless loop of failed relationships. I did not want to reside in that category. Like the old adage says, "To get different results, you must do things differently." Something needed to change, and I needed to understand what that something was. In the end my failed relationships provided a road map for finding the meaning of love.

As I wrote earlier, I had known for years that I was dealing with complex trauma. After researching the healing process, I understood the basic tenets of what I needed. A big piece was the fact that I needed to create emotional safety for myself and not continue the cycle of abuse. I had taken proactive steps to heed those guidelines by ending my previous relationships. In 2016 I began exploring a controversial and unique healing modality for people with trauma. A good friend who knew my history had shared information about an illegal plant-based medicine called psylocibin. Numerous research studies have indicated that psylocibin can bring deep healing for people with trauma. At first, I was reluctant to take an illegal drug. In addition to my concern regarding the legal ramifications, my body had always been very sensitive to strong medications, and I was concerned about the effect such a drug might have on me. However, as time went by and I continued to experience strong triggers and emotions from my trauma, I pondered the fact that I had tried just about everything else and still had not completed my healing. My years of talk therapy had definitely been helpful to a point, and I am grateful for how I was able to heal through the help of excellent therapists. However, I sensed deeper work still needed to be done, so I continued to learn about psylocibin.

In the summer of 2017, about a year after my friend had first told me about the healing effects of psylocibin, I made the decision to try the experiment for myself. I did not take lightly the fact that I would be using an illegal substance, but I was willing to try it because I had spent many years in deep pain, and I wanted healing more than anything. My reasoning was that if I or someone I loved had a painful or fatal disease and I knew of an illegal cure, I would do anything to access that solution. I intuitively knew that my freedom depended on my subconscious emotional healing.

In September 2017 I proceeded with my psylocibin experiment. My friend who was well acquainted with the use of the medicine stayed with me during my journey, which lasted between three and four hours. I kept my eyes closed the entire time as I laid still in a reclined position. The effect of the medicine gradually guided me inward over the course of the first hour as I listened to calm music.

Although words fall far short of describing how I felt, the best way I can describe the most intense part of my journey during the second and third hour is the sensation of pure love. The essence of my journey's message enabled me to actually *feel* how much I am cherished by the Universe. The energy permeated and flowed through my body from head to toe in gentle waves, like the gentle ebb and flow of the ocean tide. In my mind I saw beautiful colors flowing with the energy.

The pure loving energy spoke to me that every moment of my life had been witnessed, I had never been alone, and I was loved more than I could know. I felt completely loved and safe, like I have never felt before in my life. Those two pieces, safety and love, were all I had ever wanted. Those were the elusive pieces I had been chasing for five long and painful decades. My soul felt overwhelming joy and relief as I finally *felt* what I had wanted all my life. I cried through at least half of the journey.

In the days that followed I reflected on my life-changing experience and comprehended the most important piece that had eluded me regarding my relationship history with men, the deep piece that I needed to fully understand my vulnerability and attraction to the same type of man. I truly had been subconsciously driven my entire life as if I was in a trance.

The subconscious driving force for me in all of my relationships with men, starting with Dad, was the desire to feel safe and loved. Connected to that deep desire was the subconscious Snow White fantasy that had imprinted me with the belief that I needed a man to feel safe and loved. Because the first man from whom I had sought those emotional pieces was Dad, his energetic frequency became my subconscious template for the type of man from whom I would seek safety and love during my adult years. Unknowingly I was driven relentlessly just like an addict pursuing her fix. I had literally been looking for love in all the wrong places.

Try to imagine a young girl's emotional radar being set to constantly seek out love and safety from a specific male energetic frequency before she even knows her radar is being programmed. That image is how I have come to understand the roots of my long and painful history of destructive choices and vulnerability with men.

In addition to my relentless Dad addiction, the elements of the Bible and Mom as my role model had virtually guaranteed my lifelong prison sentence with a man like

Dad. If I had not dared to enter counseling, if Violet and Jasmine had not intervened and given me the motivation to pursue freedom and if I had not received my journey's revelation by experimenting with psylocibin, I am convinced I would still be imprisoned.

After my journey, I had clarity about needing to change my habitual relationship patterns. I needed to follow the Universe's guidance system. Now that I knew I was safe and loved in the energy that surrounded me at all times, I no longer needed to perform for or submit to a man to feel safe and loved. I felt that burden lift and my walk to freedom felt lighter and brighter as a result.

I consistently cultivated my awareness of love and tried to base my choices on that reality every day. I was slowly learning to live differently, and the Universe did not magically do the work of making different choices for me. I was responsible for making choices based on the truth I have been given.

My old programming and the addictive feelings that had controlled me for more than 50 years did not just disappear. Like most addicts with their drug, cravings for another unhealthy man like Dad surfaced now and then. I had to confront those cravings and recognize that path would not lead me to love and safety. I experienced a few temptations and had one major relapse before I was finally willing to admit to myself the depth of my addiction.

My relapse occurred a few months after my journey. The temptation appeared through the process of my house remodel. This is a very hard experience for me to write about due to the extreme shame and pain I felt afterward, yet the pain offered me the precious gift of truth, for which I am grateful to this day.

Over the course of my remodel, I became friends with the contractor, Eddie. From the beginning Eddie told me he was engaged which I told myself meant he was off limits. However, when addiction is involved, I have come to understand that nothing is really off limits. I thought I had kicked my addiction to men like my Dad, and I became too confident about my own ability to resist my drug.

Like Dad, Eddie presented with macho energy. His favorite hobbies were hunting and fishing, he loved sports, and turned on the charm when he wanted something. Over the course of months and many interactions with Eddie, my subconscious programming gradually took hold. In hindsight I know the Universe engineered that situation to show me the depth of my addiction and the extreme importance of my remaining vigilant.

When Eddie began insinuating that he would like to be more than friends, I told him that was not possible because he was engaged. He told me he was unhappy with his fiancé and was planning to end their relationship, so I foolishly agreed to meet him for lunch one day when invited. In essence, I fell for my old addiction like Snow White fell for the appeal of the old woman and her poisoned apple. I went back to sleep.

We enjoyed our meal and a few drinks. I did not succumb to Eddie's charms on that day, but the door had been opened for something more. Another day a few weeks later he dropped by my house and we had a few beers. One thing led to another. Looking back, I fully acknowledge I willingly surrendered myself to the perfect setup for my addiction to take over. After months of flirting with temptation, my willpower was pretty much zero.

I continued to see Eddie and had sex with him on several more occasions. I finally realized I needed to stop the madness, and I told him I would not be with him again because he was engaged. That was my next mistake. I kept the door wide open for more pain. He concocted the perfect plan to draw me in, and I fell for his scheme.

In December 2017 Eddie told me he had left his fiancé. He asked if he could temporarily move some of his things into my house and stay for a few nights until he found another place to stay. Tragically, I agreed. I assumed he had ended his relationship and I chose to have sex with him again. A few days later I left to go out of town.

When I returned after five days, his truck was still parked in front of my house and his belongings still there, but he was nowhere to be seen. After nine months of frequent contact, he would not answer my phone calls or texts. When he finally responded by text, he informed me that he had made a mistake and he needed to take his things from my house. He offered no further explanation.

That was my excruciating wake-up call.

After he removed his belongings from my house, I tried to contact Eddie for an explanation and soon realized that he had blocked my phone number. I never talked to or saw him again. After months of grooming me to get what he wanted, he left me feeling as if I had never mattered to him at all.

As I sat with the excruciating pain and shame resulting from how I had allowed one more man to use me, I called a "come to Jesus" meeting with myself and got real. I asked the Universe to show me what I needed to do to learn from one more painful experience and move forward. Immediately I knew I needed to accept the painful truth of my addiction and choose to be grateful for the gift from the Universe.

In January 2018, I picked myself up yet again and tweaked my Team Herps profile. By then I knew what pure love felt like and I also knew I did not need a man to feel loved. However, what I did need practice in learning was how to hold the standard for what I wanted with men. I also needed a lot of practice with loving and respecting myself in a relationship with a man. The search for my prince had become secondary to those higher goals for myself.

Over the next five months, I dated a few guys and for the most part did a noteworthy job of holding my boundaries for kindness and respect. In late May of 2018, I felt satisfied that I had made significant progress in terms of my goals and also felt in need of a reprieve from Team Herps. With a few more weeks left of my paid membership, I decided to stay open to possibilities until my membership expired on June 10. I felt good about setting that deadline if my prince had not made his appearance by then.

The morning of June 8 I checked my profile and saw no new activity other than the quirky profile of a guy who had checked out my profile and done a fly by. I am a big fan of anything quirky and my attention was drawn to his profile pic of a meme with Batman flying on a unicorn. I liked the vibe.

Although Batman had not posted any photos other than the quirky meme, my first impression from his profile was positive. He wrote well with more than just a few lines, like he had actually taken time and put thought into his profile. Very nice. He claimed to be an extreme animal lover like me, and he reportedly practiced meditation and took care of himself physically. All good signs.

Batman showed some serious potential, so on the morning of Friday, June 8, I sent him a message. I told him I liked his profile and that Batman flying on a unicorn was impressive. I informed him I would be in his area visiting my son and his wife during the coming weekend and would like to get together if he had any free time. I basically threw a hail Mary pass two days before my exit from Team Herps.

Batman responded fairly quickly by saying the timing of my visit to his area was very fortuitous (great word) and he would love to meet with me. Right on Batman. We then exchanged phone numbers and real names. I learned that Batman's alias was Clark. He made the first move by calling me that evening and we had a great conversation. We arranged to meet at a coffee shop on Sunday, June 10.

The fortuitous day of our meeting turned out to be the same day I had planned to take my sabbatical from Team Herps. I arrived at the coffee shop just before noon and sat outside on a bench. As Clark came walking around a corner, I stood up to greet him. We each grabbed a warm beverage and enjoyed conversation as we strolled for a few hours. We then stopped for lunch, enjoyed more conversation and strolled some more. We ended the day with dinner and more conversation. By then we had covered many topics. I had been honest with him about my past relationships, the reasons they had ended, and the ways in which I was trying to heal and live differently as a result of all I had learned.

As with other men before him, I shared about how anger and control were the main behaviors that were strong triggers for me. I told him that peace and healing were my top priorities and I would not sacrifice those for a relationship. Clark in turn was candid with me about his relationship history and said he was on the same page regarding peace and healing. He had an authentic energy that I had not encountered with other men.

Our day together was relaxed and simple, yet profound. Clark was respectful and kind, which were the two non-negotiable qualities I had listed for my prince. He was also very enthusiastic about and supportive of my roles as mother and grandmother, which were also among the top non-negotiables. Clark and I carried on a long-distance relationship for about nine months and began living together in April 2019. Since, then we have experienced a lot of growth, healing and gratitude together. We have been on the same page in regard to healing and peace since the day we met.

When either of us struggle we repeatedly go back to that foundation and make intentional choices to do whatever is necessary to honor our priorities and one another. When we communicate, Clark listens to me, even though he may not always understand my feelings. He shows me love and cares about me through his choices, not merely his words.

The bottom line is that Clark has consistently shown me respect and kindness every day. He lives in ways that show he genuinely cares about me. He truly is my prince.

I will always be delighted with the fact that the Universe brought my prince to me as Batman, flying on a unicorn, which just goes to show that anything can happen when we do our part and keep our hearts open. Yet more than anything Snow White learned once and for all that she did not need a prince to awaken her from the trance. The good news is that by the time she met her prince, she was fully awake. She knew she did not need him to save her. She knew that she did not need him to make her feel safe and loved. Snow White had rewritten her story.

FREEDOM

In her book, *Something More: Excavating Your Authentic Self*[19], author Sarah Ban Breathnach states, "As with driving through a patch of dark fog that comes upon you suddenly, if you keep your heart steady in the same way you would firmly hold the steering wheel, you can make it until the fog lifts. Suddenly you can see the road again. You can see where you're headed. You are returning to your Self."

That quote accurately describes the next phase of my journey to freedom. I had kept my heart steady on my long walk to freedom and the thick, dark fog started to lift. I was returning to my authentic, whole self and to freedom.

To kick off the new era, I followed through with something radical that I had contemplated for years. The issue was once again my hair. I had started going grey in my 20's and had been coloring my hair since then. At 53, I did not want to bother with that process any longer and decided to

---

[19] Something More: Excavating Your Authentic Self, 2000

go with my natural grey. The fastest and easiest way to make the extreme change was to shave my head. When I contemplated the drastic measure, I felt excitement and fear. I definitely wanted the freedom to be G.I. Jane, yet my identity had been connected to my dark hair all my life and I struggled to relinquish that part of my identity. The fear of the unknown was my barrier. What would I look like? What would other people think? Would Clark still love me? I did not want to base any decisions, even about my hair, on fear. I came to the conclusion that I needed to embrace my authentic self, grey hair and all.

My hairstylist of 16 years who had expertly helped me navigate all the stages of my hair evolution, shaved my hair down to a quarter of an inch. I loved watching her move the clippers around my head as much as I loved the scene in G.I. Jane when Demi Moore bravely takes the clippers and does the job herself. I had finally taken the leap and the feeling of freedom was absolutely fantastic. For the first time in my life, I felt authentic, no performing or pretending.

At that point I felt sure all the thick, dark fog had finally been dispelled. What I did not yet understand was that there were parts of me still hiding due to fear. Those parts of me had remained hidden as long as I was still in contact with any abuser from my past who had not acknowledged and taken full responsibility for their abuse. By the beginning of 2019 I had disconnected from every individual who fit into that category. That year would prove to be when all the terrified and wounded parts of myself finally felt safe enough to emerge into the light.

In February 2019 I enrolled in a class as part of my master's program and the first assignment required me to write a paper answering the question, "How Do You Come to Know Freedom?" Since pursuing freedom had been a passion of mine for more than a decade, I thoroughly enjoyed writing that paper. During the next class, my professor announced that she would like anyone who was willing to read their paper out loud in front of the class to do so. The entire class of 25 students sat in silence. Although I did not want to volunteer, the voice inside me that had guided me on my long walk to freedom nudged me to share my story.

I read my paper aloud, expressing how I had been raised with distorted religious programming that locked me in an emotional prison and pattern of submission and obedience to emotionally abusive men for most of my life. I shared how I became aware of the emotional abuse in 2004 and, in spite of opposition and fear, started taking steps to dig myself out of my dark prison. I spoke of how I had to break free of the terror of God's punishment in my pursuit of freedom.

My last sentences were, "In the end I learned I had to set myself free. This is how I have come to know freedom."

The class responded graciously with applause and I felt a little surprised by their kindness. For so long I had been afraid to speak my truth in fear of some kind of angry judgment or punishment. That was the first time in my life that I had spoken my story in front of total strangers. My heart was pounding.

A few other students shared their papers in class after I shared mine. I was grateful and touched to hear of their experiences and how they had come to know freedom. At the end of the class that night, our professor encouraged all of us to go one step further by reading our papers to audition for a campus-wide performance. The writing assignment about freedom had been assigned to every student on campus and anyone could sign up to audition.

The judges would choose 10 students who would then share their stories in the campus auditorium about how they had come to know freedom. As soon as I heard my professor's announcement, I felt excited and terrified all at the same time. I intuitively sensed the audition was an opportunity I needed to pursue. I was not eager to speak in front of a large audience and yet I sensed that deeper healing would come from speaking my story out loud. I wanted healing more than anything else, so I took a deep breath and signed up for the audition.

Several weeks later I read my paper in front of four members of the audition committee. When I finished speaking, they applauded and offered encouraging comments. As with my classmates, I really appreciated their kind response. The head of the committee asked how I felt after reading my paper.

"Pretty emotional," I responded.

With a kind smile, he said, "Would you be willing to memorize your paper for the presentation?"

His question took my breath away and for a few seconds I considered my answer. In spite of feeling completely overwhelmed at the thought, I smiled and calmly said, "Sure." I sounded way more confident that I felt.

After I thanked the committee for the opportunity to audition, I was told that I would receive an email within a week letting me know if I had been chosen. Although I wanted to participate for the sake of my healing, I also felt peace in letting go of the outcome. I knew if I was meant to speak, I would be chosen, and I completely let go and trusted the Universe to determine the outcome.

The next week I received an email informing me that I had been selected as one of the 10 students to speak for the big event. Once again, combined feelings of excitement and terror washed over me. I had about six weeks to memorize my paper, which would ultimately amount to six or seven minutes in length. Except for minor performances during my youth, I had not spoken anything by memory in my life, let alone in front of a large audience. I remembered the encouraging adage, "How do you eat an elephant? One bite at a time." I commenced my mental recording, one bite at a time.

The process of memorizing and speaking my story catalyzed powerful inner transformation. The truth of my story became much more real each time I heard myself speaking the words out loud. Even during the process of memorizing the words by myself, I was changed. Although my memories and emotions had always remained a part of me, I had not been able to feel most of them. They had literally been buried alive for all those years.

The process of repeatedly speaking about my pain, even when alone, started the slow process of seeing, feeling and accepting my truth. I realized at a certain point, even before I stood before an audience, that the process was not first about telling my truth to other people. The process was first about telling the truth to myself. More than anyone, I needed to know the truth. The voices inside of me had been silenced and imprisoned for too long. The time had come for all of my terrified parts to emerge from the darkness and speak their truth in the light.

For the first time in my life, I began to truly listen to and embrace the silenced parts of myself, the parts from whom I had dissociated. As I spoke my truth out loud over and over, I was hit with wave upon wave of fear, pain and grief.

The night of the presentation rolled around, and I felt as ready as I would ever feel. I had rehearsed my story in front of Clark several times. Although speaking my truth in front of him was difficult, the voices of my traumatized self would bow to fear no longer. They were determined to be heard. *She* was determined to be heard.

I walked on stage in front of approximately 300 audience members in March 2019. My voice was calm and resolute. I spoke with confidence and allowed every word of my story to be heard. Freedom came to my imprisoned parts that night. The audience gave me a standing ovation and I stood in awe of their kindness. Freedom, freedom at last!

I thought my speech was the final breakthrough and

that I would never again be shackled by my trauma wounds but when I returned home that night, the all-too-familiar voices of my programming tried to paralyze me once again. As I tried to relax and go to sleep, I began to experience unbridled terror. All the voices of my past rose up, voices threatening me with punishment because I had openly spoken my truth. Intense panic rushed through me, and I began thinking irrational thoughts such as signing up for witness protection program to remain safe. I know that sounds ludicrous and yet that was how terrified I had always been of the religious system and the people who had abused me. I felt like they would do anything and everything to silence me and I did not know what reaction to expect.

Eventually my fearful thoughts subsided. A few weeks passed without being struck down by lightning or any other form of punishment, and I felt fairly confident that most of my healing path was behind me.

In April 2019 I began sensing impressions for the need of another journey with psylocibin, which came as a surprise since I felt I had completed my healing process with my speech. I felt intuitively guided to contact my oldest daughter, Sara, who was currently living by herself in the one room log cabin built by Edward in 1980, where he had lived on Mac and Marion's property when I first met him.

Although the thought of returning to that property triggered a great deal of fear and dread, I felt clearly guided to have my journey in that location. The cabin represented Edward and his energy, as well as his parents. I understood why the location was so important, knowing that the roots of my trauma with him began there. In spite of my fear, I knew beyond a shadow of a doubt that I would receive healing, although I had no idea of how the process would unfold.

Clark accompanied me to the cabin which was the only building left of the original residences on Mac and Marion's property. Interestingly, Mac and Marion's ornate Swiss chalet on the river had been torn down just a month before by the current landowner to make way for a new home. When I arrived at the cabin, I saw a beautiful, translucent geodome that Sara had built amidst the tall pines. She offered that beautiful space to me for my journey, and I expressed overwhelming gratitude for her gesture of love.

The journey that unfolded in that space was very different than the first. This time I was guided deeper into the pain and terror that I had buried and blocked out for decades. The levels of pain and fear I had suppressed were intense, which explained my complex trauma and the severe triggers that blindsided me if anything reminded me of Edward or the years when I was imprisoned. I also received the clear message that all of my pain had resulted from basing choices on fear. Fear of anger, loss of emotional connection and most of all, fear of God's punishment.

My journey ended with a vision of me in a crouched position, hiding in the back corner of a dark prison cell that resembled a cave. That was a portrayal of the thick, dark fog where all my traumatized parts had hidden for decades. Someone entered the space and I cried out in terror, crouching even lower, shielding my head with my hands. The intensity of the pain and fear in that moment were what I felt the first time I was sexually assaulted and every time since then, including all the years of my marriage. The common denominator in all of those circumstances was that I was given no voice and no choice by the men who used me. I had therefore dissociated from my feelings many times and buried the pain in order to survive. The emotional pain and terror I felt during those few moments of my journey was severe and paralyzing.

The next instant my eyes opened involuntarily, and I gazed up at the blue skies and white clouds above me. I will never forget the sheer beauty of that moment. I heard the sound of the birds. I saw the giant pine trees towering above me. Although my senses took a few minutes to fully grasp reality, I knew that my prison cell was open. I was free. The thick, dark fog had been dispelled. That glorious moment was like opening my eyes and feeling freedom for the first time.

In the days and weeks that followed I continued to absorb the reality that the only way I could remain free was not to base my choices on fear. The journey at the cabin and my speech at the university went hand in hand. Speaking my story in front of an audience had enabled me to open up and comprehend my truth on a deeper level, giving voice to my true self.

The journey at the cabin had enabled me to open up emotionally and begin absorbing the full depth of emotion I had suppressed for decades. Both parts were necessary in order for me to see, embrace and reclaim every part of myself. I no longer wanted or needed to hide.

After decades of involuntary coping mechanisms, all of my authentic parts were finally, slowly integrating into my conscious awareness. I was becoming my whole self for the first time in my life. However, as I had experienced before, I would receive another clear impression guiding me to take yet another step for healing.

A month after my geodome journey, I traveled back to the place where I was born. In May 2019, I gazed upon the legendary Lake Superior – the largest body of fresh water in the world. On a summer day in 1965 I had been born into and immersed in that powerful energy. Almost 54 years later, I had returned to once again immerse myself for the purpose of healing. I felt awe struck by the immensity of the lake, the appearance of which looked just like the ocean with the tide rolling in on the shore.

Down through history, waves have been recorded at 30 feet high and winds at 90 miles an hour have furiously swept across the lake. Most of us have heard of the lake's danger, with more than 350 shipwrecks recorded throughout history. I felt thrilled as I sensed the water's energy, knowing that I had begun my journey on earth cradled by that power.

Before I traveled, I had felt impressed to make an appointment with an energy healer specifically trained in the shamanic practice of soul retrieval. Prior to my trip I had no previous experience with a shaman. In fact, I had not even thought about an appointment with a shaman until

I visited her website a few weeks prior for the purpose of finding a massage therapist, when I noticed she also offered sessions in shamanic soul retrieval. The basic premise of soul retrieval is that whenever we experience trauma, a part of our vital essence, or soul, separates from us in order to survive the experience by escaping the full impact of the pain. This quiet occurrence, known as soul loss, takes the form of a perpetual feeling and experience of incompleteness and disconnection, which was exactly how I had felt since I was a child. I sensed this was the reason I had been guided to travel back to my birthplace. My healing process required me to return in order to retrieve the lost parts of myself and regain wholeness.

My soul retrieval session was scheduled during an afternoon in late May 2019. That morning, in preparation for the session, I followed through with something the Universe had guided me to do. During the week before I left, I felt clearly impressed to take two specific pieces of jewelry with me – my wedding ring and a bracelet. Those beautiful pieces had been tucked away in the back recesses of my dresser and I had not worn them for years. They both represented deep emotional connections to my marriage.

The morning before my soul retrieval session, I walked out to the tip of a small peninsula of land which extends out into the lake. I sat on a large rock above the water and absorbed the calm, healing energy of Lake Superior. I reflected on the Snow-White dreams I had at the beginning of my marriage and the depth of pain and trauma I had accumulated instead. I took one last look at the emotionally charged pieces of jewelry and surrendered them to the lake.

I stayed seated on the rock, breathing deeply to release the pain. Eight years after my divorce, I did not foresee that letting go of the final connections to my dream would be so painful. Gradually I felt calm and strong enough to walk away and open myself to my soul retrieval session.

When I arrived at my appointment, the shaman guided me to her quiet seating area and asked me why I had come to see her.

I presented her with a photo of myself as a two-day old baby in the town hospital, lying next to a pillow with the name of the hospital stamped in black ink on the pillowcase.

"I have been guided to you for healing," I told her. "I was born here almost 54 years ago, and my family left when I was two years old."

As we sat together, she explained the shamanic healing process to me.

"Shamanism is an ancient collection of traditions based on accessing and connecting to spirit realms for wisdom and healing. Shamanic practitioners call on compassionate helping spirits to assist in healing, restoring spiritual power and helping clients return to wholeness. During your session I will use a drum and rattle and will journey to the spirit realm for the purpose of restoring and removing energetic pathways, recovering soul parts, and communicating with spirits."

Upon hearing her explanation of the shamanic process, I knew more than I ever that I was in the right place. She then led me into an adjacent room and instructed me to lay face up on the massage table. She asked me to turn my attention inward while keeping my eyes closed. After about five minutes of deep breathing while gentle, soothing music played in the background, she began the soul retrieval process.

My mind sunk into a deep inner realm. The session lasted about an hour and a half, and the time passed quickly. I heard the sounds of rattles and drums as well as chanting and blowing. The sounds seemed distant, like surface sounds would seem to a diver under water. When the shaman gradually brought the session to a close, she quietly instructed me to slowly come back to present moment awareness. After five or ten minutes, I joined her in the sitting area, and she explained to me what had happened during my soul retrieval.

"Your 34-year-old Self brought your 2-year-old Self back to you. What was happening at the time you were 34?" she asked.

I reflected on that part of my life 20 years before and realized that we moved to Arizona that year.

I told her, "That was the very beginning of my long healing journey to freedom. I was also the mother of four children with my youngest being two years old at the time."

She then continued her explanation of my healing process. "There were numerous energetic cords attached to you, all of which I severed. One was especially strong, and I had to return several times to completely sever that one."

She and I talked about how the energy of our abusers, especially sexual, can remain connected to us long after the abuse is over. Their energy can affect our emotional body like a physical parasite would affect our physical body keeping us in a weakened energetic state, thereby blocking our ability to heal and be free.

As with a physical parasite, outside intervention is often necessary to remove the energetic cords. Her perspective resonated as true in terms of all the men who had used and abused me. I believe the strongest energetic cord which required the most time and energy to sever was Edward's, as a result of his abuse over the course of our marriage.

As I sat with the shaman and reflected on what she had told me, I felt I had been changed on a soul level. I was no longer the same woman I had been when I walked through her door. My soul retrieval session had returned a large part of my authentic self, enabling me to be whole and free for the first time in my life.

Abusive energies were no longer attached to, controlling and weakening me. My performer and codependent self, as strong and as necessary as she had been for my survival, no longer needed to be in control. From that moment on my authentic self would remain front and center. She would base her choices not on fear, but on freedom. The path ahead would be the path of freedom she had been destined to walk since she took her first breath along the shore of Lake Superior.

Despite the fact that I had blocked out a great deal of my lived experience, the reintegration of those parts still felt familiar because they had always been a part of me. On some level we had always been connected. I do not expect anyone else to believe or accept those parts of me. What matters is that *I* accept and embrace those parts of me. Each and every emotion I had felt since birth, ranging from loneliness to terror to agonizing pain to deep grief to fiery rage, I now accept and embrace my *whole self* with unconditional love and compassion. That is the simple and yet profound reason why I have healing and freedom today. While I strongly believe "You can't heal what you can't feel," those feelings can take their toll. Over the months that followed my shamanic soul retrieval I struggled with the heavy emotions connected to all the times I had dissociated. By February of 2020 I felt impressed to seek help. Not only had I surrendered to and embraced all the parts of myself that had been silenced for decades in the fog I began living with their full emotional reality every day. I still experienced deep grief and anxiety from the trauma that had occurred during my childhood and marriage. The emotional weight was almost paralyzing at times. By far my greatest pain and sorrow came from the awareness that I had surrendered my precious self to men who did not care about me and had only used me for their pleasure. That thought alone broke my heart.

For years I had done everything I knew of to care for and love myself including regular exercise, meditation, mantras, deep breathing, reducing stress, eating well, cultivating gratitude for all my blessings and staying connected to loving family and friends. Although all those efforts definitely brought healing, I sensed I needed more help. I was up against a weight I could not shift myself.

I made an appointment with my doctor and for the first time in my life discussed the possibility of taking medication for depression and anxiety. She prescribed a low dose of one she thought would be helpful and I am very grateful to say I felt improvement after a few weeks. Since then, I have consistently felt a significant reduction in the emotional heaviness and much less anxiety in connection with my trauma.

People who know me well have also noticed a significant difference. I acknowledge that medication may not be the best choice for everyone, and we all need to be careful when turning to pharmaceuticals of any kind, yet I also want to be real about how I have personally been helped through this intervention. We need to be open and willing to ask for help.

There are no words to adequately express my gratitude to the Universe for all the countless times and ways I have been powerfully helped and guided along my healing journey. All through the years I have consistently been given the necessary courage, assistance and resources every step of the way. I truly know that in my darkest moments I was never alone.

I began my life journey on this planet with subconscious programming that taught me to believe I could only receive love and safety through obeying out of fear. I was mercilessly driven to perform, believing I had to obediently submit without regard for my feelings or my well-being.

Thanks to many years of healing, I no longer live controlled by my programming or by other people, and I am free from abuse in the name of God. The truth has set me free. Today Snow White is fully awake, living and breathing in the pure love, light and healing of the Universe. I live every day as we are all meant to live. In FREEDOM.

EPILOGUE

I express my sincere gratitude to everyone who has chosen to read my story. I truly appreciate you taking your valuable time and energy to listen. I can only speak for myself when I say this has truly been a healing, freeing experience. I hope you are able to say the same. I have learned that no matter where we are or where we have been, every moment is an opportunity to walk toward healing and freedom.

If I could pass on just one piece of advice from my journey, I encourage you to do everything within your power to pursue freedom and not base choices on fear. As has been true for me, your journey to freedom may take years. I encourage you to embrace the truth that every day, every step and every choice matter. If you are experiencing or have experienced abuse and trauma, please ask for help by pursuing avenues of healing such as counseling, energy work, and environments that provide you with emotional and physical safety. Healing is possible. I am living proof.

If anyone tries to use the name of God or the Bible to control, use, abuse or exploit you, ask for help or walk away. The pure loving energy of the Universe will never control, use, abuse or exploit anyone. The Universe will never insist that we perform or jump through hoops to earn love or acceptance and will certainly never control us through fear or terror. The Universe offers love freely to anyone who opens their heart to receive, regardless of their history or past choices.

If you are a person who has used or is currently using religion, the Bible or fear to control, use, abuse or exploit another person, please examine your choices. Understand that instead of doing damage you have the ability to make different choices that will lead to healing and freedom.

In September of 2020 the Universe offered me another healing opportunity. My mom passed away unexpectedly at the age of 88, during the writing of this book. I am deeply grateful to say that I received healing and peace in my relationship with her during her final days.

In August of 2020 I had spent time with Mom when Violet, Clark and I traveled to Montana for a visit. At that time, she was still living in her own home where she had chosen to live by herself for 20 years, cherishing her independence. We enjoyed our visit with her that weekend.

The Sunday afternoon when we were leaving, as I was getting into the car, I looked back at Mom standing in front of her house, holding onto the railing. As had been the case in previous years, my heart ached as I saw her standing there so frail, not knowing if I would see her again. A clear

voice inside me said *Go back and give her one more hug.*
I walked back and held her in my arms, feeling overwhelming love for her as I pressed her frail, bony body
against mine. During that brief hug I felt all the deep love
I had felt for her all of my life. Those few precious moments
will forever be imprinted on my heart. Just as I had expressed to her frequently in letters and phone calls, I told
her I loved her very much. She told me I was very special
to her and she loved me. We held each other for a few more
seconds, gave each other a kiss, and I walked back to the
car in tears. That was the last time I saw her in her cherished, independent setting.

A few weeks later I called her for a phone visit. Shortly
into our conversation she shared that she had fallen nine
days earlier, resulting in neck pain, two black eyes, purple
lips, and bruising on her face. She told me that for the first
time in her life she had visited a chiropractor. I felt very
concerned after hearing about the severity of her injuries,
yet she assured me that she had another appointment with
the chiropractor in a few days and she had been in close
contact with her naturopathic consultant who had cared
for her for years.

Despite my concern, I knew better than to try to convince Mom to seek additional medical help, so I did not
pressure her into seeing a traditional doctor. Since Dad's
passing more than 20 years prior, her independent spirit
had been fierce, and she was always intent on making her
own decisions. Also, as she had done my entire life, she continued to quote Bible verses to claim her healing.

Four days later I received a phone call from Ted's wife, Diane, who lived close to Mom. She had been keeping in close contact with Mom to make sure she was safe. Sadly, Diane had discovered Mom lying on her kitchen floor where she had been immobile after falling again almost 20 hours before. This time, Mom was taken to the hospital where tests showed two fractures in her pelvis and a fracture in her neck at C2.

To prevent paralysis, Mom was placed in a restrictive, metal brace that kept her neck and head stable. Over the days following her admission to the hospital, the doctors discussed her prognosis for recovery. Due to the fact that she was very thin and had severe osteoporosis, the likelihood of her bones healing was minimal to none. Despite this information, Mom wanted to try a regimen of physical therapy in order to regain the ability to walk and return home. The doctors agreed to honor her decision.

Shortly after Mom had been admitted to the hospital her inability to swallow food or liquid became clear. A modified barium swallowing test revealed that she was aspirating at least half of what she attempted to swallow into her lungs. This impairment resulted from the fracture in her neck and precipitated pneumonia during her second day in the hospital. The doctors then recommended a feeding tube be inserted through her nose into her stomach in order to give her nutrition and the necessary strength to participate in physical therapy.

Mom agreed to the feeding tube in hopes of being able to walk again. After 36 hours with the feeding tube inserted and several sessions of physical therapy, she decided that both were too painful. After consulting with her doctor, she made the decision to discontinue receiving nutrition or hydration and be kept comfortable for the remainder of her life. When Diane informed me of Mom's decision, I postponed my school commitments and traveled to be with her the following day. Although Clark and my kids offered to travel to Montana to be with me and Mom, I sensed that I needed to have time alone with her. Another detail affecting my decision involved the Covid regulations which restricted the number of visitors allowed to see Mom. I arrived at the hospital the next evening. Only one or two visitors were allowed in Mom's room at a time between 9 o'clock in the morning and 9 o'clock at night. Each day Diane kindly informed me when I could visit Mom. Other family members were scheduled in shifts throughout the day as well.

Upon entering her hospital room that first evening, I had no idea how much longer Mom would be alive. I wanted to make sure the time we had together was as happy and peaceful as possible. Despite the fact that Diane informed me of Mom's specific request that no one bring her flowers, I brought her a mixed bouquet which contained several coral-colored roses. I felt confident that she would forgive my disobedience based on her responses to many bouquets I had given her over the years on her birthdays, Christmas and Mother's Day. She had always been delighted with the gift of flowers.

She was sleeping when I entered the room. At the first

sight of her frail appearance, like a skeleton with skin, my heart broke. All I wanted to do was love her. Every ounce of me wished I could wave a magic wand and heal her broken body. I touched her hand and kissed her on the forehead. Her eyes opened and when she saw me, her face lit up with a huge smile. I will never forget that smile and the beautiful love I felt between us.

During our first night together, I suggested she could talk to my kids and grandkids via FaceTime video calls if she felt strong enough, and she eagerly agreed. She had always enjoyed her phone visits with them, and especially loved whenever they were able to travel with me to Montana.

During each FaceTime call that night, Mom was fully coherent and able to converse although her voice was weak, and her speech somewhat slurred. She even managed to give mini-sermons about the importance of faith and the Bible during her 10-minute phone visits with each of them, which did not surprise them or me at all. Her sermons had always been a predictable part of their life experience with her. All in all, the phone visits were filled with love and gratitude, and everyone was grateful to have that last conversation.

During my conversation with Mom that night, she asked me several direct questions about my relationship with Clark. Although I had spoken with her several times regarding the subject, telling her that Clark and I agree regarding our spiritual beliefs, she once again wanted to know how I would integrate my faith while in a relationship with a Buddhist. I respectfully reminded her of the fact that, as I had told her before, I believe in a Universal source of love which is available to all people, regardless of faith and religious beliefs. She responded by quietly saying, "Okay."

She then inquired as to whether or not Clark and I would choose to be married. I told her we had talked about the subject and if we ever did choose to take that step, we would agree on the right time. After living through long, difficult marriages and divorces, neither of us wanted to rush into anything. Again, she quietly said, "Okay."

I reemphasized to her that Clark is the kindest, most respectful man I have known, and I am very grateful to have him as my partner. I told her I am no longer subject to anger or punishing silence as I had been for so many years in my marriage. She quickly identified with that comment, nodding her head and saying, "I lived with a lot of that too."

That was the first time I had heard such transparency about her marriage, and I told her, "I know, Mom, and I'm sorry that was true. You deserved kindness and respect."

Years before, after Dad had passed away in 1998, she and I had briefly discussed Dad's volatile anger, especially in light of my car accident when I was a teenager and how we had both cried because we were so afraid to tell him. After recounting that story, I specifically asked her how his volatile anger affected her.

"Were you afraid of Dad's anger?"

She paused and responded, "Yes."

I followed up by asking her, "Did you feel like you were

walking on eggshells around him?"

Again, she paused reflectively and responded, "Yes, I suppose so."

Her brief moments of honesty back then and again in her hospital room gave me deeper understanding of her, myself and my childhood. Following my comment about her deserving kindness and respect, she redirected the conversation by emphasizing that Dad had been a good man with many good qualities. I did not argue with her. Her re-directing of conversations for the purpose of changing an uncomfortable subject was nothing new to me. I had experienced that dynamic with her my entire life. She would believe what she chose to believe, and I was not going to try to change her mind. I was not there to focus on our differences.

As the first evening progressed, I asked her several times if she wanted me to leave so she could rest. She replied emphatically that she did not want to sleep as long as I could stay with her. I asked if she wanted me to read the Bible to her or sing songs. She enthusiastically chose the latter. Having been the piano player at church for decades, her passion for music and worship remained strong.

For an hour we sang some old traditional hymns, some of which I had to Google to remember the lyrics. At times she closed her eyes and raised her thin arms in worship. To be honest, I had a very hard time holding my emotions in check during that hour. I fought valiantly to continue singing. Eventually I had to stop due to the fact that my emotions rendered me speechless.

Eventually, Mom fell asleep, and a nurse came in to let me know she needed to get Mom ready for the night. I kissed Mom and tearfully said goodbye to her. "I'll see you soon, Mom. I love you very much," I told her through tears.

She opened her eyes and replied, "I probably won't be here in the morning."

I said, "Okay. Either way I'll see you soon and I'll keep talking to you because I know you'll still be with me."

She nodded her head and peacefully closed her eyes.

When I stepped out of the room, I approached the nurse's station in tears and asked what I could expect in terms of Mom's passing. The nurse told me she had witnessed patients lasting between several days to two weeks without hydration or nutrition. She then informed me that Mom had pressed her intently several times the night before to give her medication to assist her in passing. She informed Mom that she could not grant her request, which made Mom upset.

The nurse told Mom they were able to give her medication to ease her pain, ranging from Tylenol to morphine. During her last days, Mom rarely requested any of those options. I asked her numerous times if she needed anything for pain and she said no. Other than the times when she asked the nurse to reposition her and the pillows, she said she did not experience any pain.

The next day I had been assigned the time frame of nine to eleven in the morning for visitation. I did not sleep well after my first visit with Mom and was awakened by the ringing of my hotel phone at 7:30 a.m.

"Hello?" I mumbled.

"Hi Honey, it's Mom."

"Hi Mom, how are you doing this morning?"

"Well, I'm hungry. Have you had breakfast yet?"

"No, I haven't had breakfast. I'll come to see you after I grab a quick bite and then we'll get you some breakfast."

I arrived at the hospital an hour later. She was sleeping and I kissed her on the forehead to wake her. When she opened her eyes and saw me, she looked surprised and stated matter-of-factly, "I didn't expect to see you again. I thought I'd be dead. I don't know how many times I can keep saying goodbye to people."

I laughed and said, "Sorry, Mom, but you're going to have to put up with me one more time."

That morning I felt so much compassion as I witnessed Mom taking great pleasure in savoring a few drops of applesauce or egg yolk. She closed her eyes, relishing each taste. The goal of her eating was not to give her body nutrition. The goal was to give her moments of delight.

After a few tiny bits of egg and applesauce, Mom told me she needed to discuss some important matters and make some big decisions that day.

She stated, "I'd like to call the assisted living place where some of my friends live."

Okay, Mom," I responded. "You'll probably need to have your feeding tube reinserted if you want to live there."

She nodded in agreement and replied, "I guess I could do that."

I texted Diane and told her about Mom's latest ideas. She responded by saying that I needed to have the doctor and the Hospice representative talk to Mom again. Shortly thereafter, they came to Mom's room and I explained to them everything that she had communicated to me about living in an assisted living facility with her friends. The doctor then proceeded to very kindly and clearly communicate to Mom everything that had transpired in the past week. As the doctor delineated the facts about her injuries and her choices to discontinue hydration and nutrition, Mom defended her latest perspective and hopes for rehabilitation by telling the doctor that "my helper applied applesauce to my forehead last night which helped quite a bit" (that 'helper' being me). The doctor gave me a knowing look, clearly communicating that Mom was not fully coherent.

Ultimately the doctor was able to bring Mom back around full circle. In spite of her valiant attempt to convince me, the doctor and the palliative care representative that she had the option of living in the assisted living facility, Mom ultimately conceded to the doctor's diagnosis and agreed to remain on comfort care for the duration of her life.

At her own request, Mom sat in her hospital chair for 20 minutes several times a day and did gentle leg and foot exercises. Only a few days before her passing, her independent spirit was alive and strong. At one point during one of my visits, she was sitting in her chair and I was sitting in front of her. She looked at me quizzically and asked, "How do you do your hair?"

I laughed and told her, "I just wash and dry it. The whole process only takes me about five or ten minutes."

She looked at me in shock, rolled her eyes, and exclaimed, "It takes me six hours to wash and dry my hair!"

"Oh no! That's terrible!" I exclaimed. "I'm so sorry to hear that!"

We laughed together and then she raised her thin arms in the air, pumped her hands up and down in a celebratory fashion, and with a big smile exclaimed, "But I won't have to do it anymore!"

That was a priceless moment. We both laughed some more, and the levity and joy felt like a cool breeze on a hot day.

During our times together she communicated her awareness of her impending death. Several different times she looked at me in genuine surprise and stated, "I'm dying." I looked at her with all the love in my heart and said, "I know, Mom." Those moments were heartbreaking.

The night before she passed, I was able to spend a few hours with her. For the most part she slept that evening. At one point she woke up and in a barely audible voice instructed me, "I want to talk to the family out there." She motioned and pointed to the empty hallway behind me, and I knew she was hallucinating.

"I'm sorry, Mom, they aren't allowed in your room right now. I'll give them a message if you'd like."

She was not appeased by my suggestion and increased the urgency of her request by stating, "I want to speak to them right now, with YOU." I again stated that I was sorry, that they could not be allowed in her room and I would gladly convey any message she wanted to give them.

She then proceeded to determinedly grab the side railing on her bed and pull herself over on her side, while attempting to swing both of her thin legs over the side of the bed. I stood in front of her, blocking her attempted exit. She looked up at me with a stern look on her face, and stated with fervor, "You need to get out of my way."

I smiled and gently replied, "I'm sorry, Mom. I can't do that."

Her irritation was obvious, and she looked at me with exasperation, defiantly stating, "Why not?"

"Because the doctor gave specific orders for you to rest so you can recover and get stronger." My well-intended deception produced the hoped-for results, and after pausing and looking at me with consternation for a few more moments, she settled back into her bed, albeit at a cock-eyes angle. She was her feisty self, right up until the end.

What I later told the nurse about Mom's fierce attempt to get out of bed, including her clear directives toward me, the nurse explained a phenomenon called the "death rally", which is often witnessed close to the end of life. A patient will display surges of energy or increased lucidity, giving the false perception of the revitalization of energy or recovery. She believed Mom's surge of energy could have been representative of this phenomenon. In hindsight, that proved to be true.

After being comfortably repositioned in her bed, Mom

slept while I sat with her for another hour, talking to her and singing. I recited the 23rd Psalm several times. I told her several things I needed to tell her.

"Mom, I'm writing a book. The purpose of the book is healing and freedom, both for me and hopefully others. I know you love me, and I love you. I know you never intended to hurt me. My story is not about blaming you or anyone else, but I need to tell the truth. I never wanted a barrier between us but there were parts of my life I could not share with you because I knew you could not understand. What I most want you to know is that I have always loved you very much and I always will."

Through many tears I said everything I needed and wanted to say to her. I felt like a million tons had been lifted off of my chest. The Universe knew I needed to speak my truth and gave me that night as my final time with Mom here on this earth. After sitting silently and holding her hand, I kissed her one more time, told her I loved her, and said goodbye in peace. I am and always will be so very grateful that I was given the precious gift of those last hours with her. Twelve hours later, she was gone.

The next morning, I prepared for my visit with Mom which was scheduled from nine to eleven. I checked in at the front desk and went through the required Covid procedures. As with prior visits, a staff member called Mom's floor to ensure that she did not have other visitors at that time. Surprisingly, I was told I could not go up to her room due to the fact that she already had two visitors in her room. I assured the staff that I was scheduled to see her at nine.

A few seconds later, my phone rang.

When I answered, Diane said tearfully, "Mom is close to passing. She asked the nurse to call for Ted and me at 7 this morning."

I caught my breath and asked through tears, "Can I come up to say goodbye?

I heard her consulting with Ted, and she replied, "Yes."

Before we had a chance to hang up, I heard someone talking to Diane and she told me, "Mom just passed away."

I stood in the hospital lobby stunned, knowing that only a few minutes had prevented me from being with Mom one more time before she passed. I immediately made my way to the elevator in the lobby. I was feeling mixed emotions as I made my way up to Mom's floor. Ted and Seth were still with Mom, so I waited in the hallway for them to leave. They walked out and past me with their eyes lowered. I went in and kissed Mom one last time on the forehead and then on the lips, which had always been her favorite way of greeting me and saying goodbye.

Someone had taken one of the coral roses from the bouquet I had given her and placed the beautiful bloom in her hands, along with a small Bible. I felt deeply grateful that she was at peace, while at the same time feeling the enormous pain of knowing that the woman whom I had loved all my life was now gone. My love for her and her love for me will carry on in my heart.

I feel her presence with me, and I know I will see her again one day. Until then I will keep right on talking to her, like I promised her I would.

AUTHOR'S NOTE

I have written this book for two reasons. First, I am compelled to do so for the sake of freedom. I believe every individual has the right to pursue their spiritual or non-spiritual path in freedom. I do not assume to judge any person's choice regarding religion or spirituality. However, if any person's beliefs result in harm to another, or their beliefs are imposed or forced on another, especially with the threat of punishment connected to noncompliance, my stance shifts from tolerance to intolerance. Such dictatorial behavior strips a person of their right to freedom.

Second, I am compelled to write this book for the sake of healing for myself and hopefully others. Several years ago, in search of truth and understanding, I came across a YouTube talk entitled *Complex Trauma: Understanding and Treatment*[20], by Dr. Diane Langberg, a psychologist who has spent 40 years working with survivors of complex trauma. Listening to her talk was the first time I truly

---

[20] Complex Trauma: Understanding and Treatment, 2016

understood the truth about myself, my past and my life. In reference to healing of complex trauma, Dr. Langberg states, "Eventually words will and must come. It's part of how you get power over something, to be able to tell it."

Writing the words on these pages has been agonizing, enlightening, and ultimately freeing. Dr. Langberg is right. Today, rather than my story having power over me as had been true for more than 50 years, I now have power over my story. I believe freedom can only be realized through truth. I am more grateful than I can say, each and every moment, for freedom.

I have chosen to use all fictional names in this book. My intention is not to blame or judge. My only intentions are truth and healing.

FREEDOM!

OHHHH! THE PURE JOY OF BEING WITH A DOG!

~ ONE YEAR OLD ~

~ SEVEN YEARS OLD ~

ACKNOWLEDGMENTS

To Julie Cantrell for her loving support and expert guidance and editing.

To Asya Blue for her brilliant and beautiful cover and book design.

To Chris Amram for his creative and inspired photography.

To Mitch Holford for his generosity in loaning me his prized motorcycle for the cover shoot.

To Dr. Diane Langberg and all the healers, living and otherwise, who have assisted me.

To Melody Beattie and Clarissa Pinkola Estes for their life-saving books.

To Rose McGowan for setting a powerful example with her memoir, Brave.

To the fabulous performer Pink, who continually inspires me and helps me understand that no matter how messy, I am F'n Perfect.

To the genius comedian Maria Bamford who always brings me healing through laughter.

To All of You... Thank You for being a part of my healing journey to freedom.

Made in the USA
Monee, IL
22 July 2021